LIBRARY SCIENCE TEXT SERIES

Library Instruction for Librarians

LIBRARY INSTRUCTION
for
LIBRARIANS

ANNE F. ROBERTS

LIBRARIES UNLIMITED, INC.
Littleton, Colorado
1982

LIBRARIES UNLIMITED, INC.
P.O. Box 263
Littleton, Colorado 80160

Library of Congress Cataloging in Publication Data

Roberts, Anne F., 1937-
   Library instruction for librarians.

   (Library science text series)
   Includes bibliographies.
   1. Library education.   2. Education, Humanistic.
I. Title.   II. Series.
Z668.R6   1982   020'.7'11   82-13997
ISBN 0-87287-298-X
ISBN 0-87287-331-5 (pbk.)

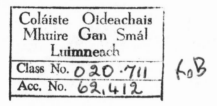
Libraries Unlimited books are bound with Type II nonwoven material that meets
and exceeds National Association of State Textbook Administrators' Type II
nonwoven material specifications Class A through E.

TABLE OF CONTENTS

LIST OF FIGURES

ACKNOWLEDGMENTS

I wish to thank Heather Cameron and Ann Hartman, editors at Libraries Unlimited, Inc., and Hannelore Rader and Carla Stoffle for their helpful advice and support. I also thank my family, Warren, Erin, James, Thomas, Peter, Buster and Sally, too, for their encouragement during the writing of the book.

INTRODUCTION

This textbook suggests a new way of looking at libraries, their services, and their users; it takes the approach that the humanistic or holistic view can restore values and traditions to libraries by focusing on users and their needs. This approach brings together the social and intellectual roles of both users and librarians and makes use of individual differences and styles in both areas. The goal of this textbook is to make library instruction accessible from humanistic means. The book is the result of a thoughtful analysis of what, over the years, has been tried and has worked. This study provides students and librarians with a theoretical and historical framework for library instruction and offers an interdisciplinary approach to the practical applications of library instruction.

Background information contained in the textbook includes a review of the literature, a discussion of the current status of library instruction, and an overview of library instruction in academic, school, public, and special libraries. Components of a library instruction plan—determining user needs, setting goals and objectives, organizing and administering the program—are discussed in detail, as are specific teaching techniques and methods of implementing library instruction activities. Various modes of library instruction, including the lecture, the group discussion, self-directed learning, one-to-one teaching, use of printed materials, audiovisual presentations, and computer-assisted instruction, are described in Chapter III, while Chapter IV examines the advantages and disadvantages of the most common methods of library instruction—formal courses, tutorials, seminars, workbooks, etc. Chapter V discusses various techniques for evaluating user performance and the effectiveness of the library instruction program. Following each of the chapters are suggested assignments and selected readings, the latter chosen for their accessibility and practicality. Appendices include model goals, guidelines, objectives, the American Library Association policy statement for instruction in the use of libraries, future recommendations for library instruction, and checklists to be used in organizing and managing a library instruction program. Guidelines for planning library instruction, sample materials for a self-guided tour, a library skills test, guides for research, and a basic course outline with worksheets and workbook exercises are incorporated into the text. In actually implementing a library instruction program, setting goals, surveying needs, and planning would be the first steps; however, since this work is designed as a text, the chapters on modes and methods of library instruction come first since the students must understand these before being able to comprehend the planning process.

The holistic approach to library instruction restores those library services which certain members of the profession have seen as disintegrating. This vision is one in which particular attention is paid to users, who take on the responsibility for meeting their own information needs, and one in which librarians are the educators/teachers/facilitators in the process. Librarianship is seen as an organic whole with libraries collecting, organizing, and delivering services and materials to users.

This textbook sketches in the outlines of what can be done in teaching library instruction for librarians, and as such is only a beginning. It has been geared mainly towards academic libraries, and it is from this source that most examples have come, since that has been the primary experience of the author. Nevertheless, the belief that libraries are similar suggests that the principles of library instruction are fundamentally the same and that the ideas and methods can be adapted from one type of library to another easily and effectively.

Library instruction has matured and come of age. The field has its own theories, objectives, modes, methods, and techniques, although more work is needed in the areas of research, evaluation, and teaching. It is hoped that future instruction librarians will move forward and continue the work of past generations of instruction librarians. In order for users to differentiate among information and distinguish between the useful and the not useful, library instruction must assume a vital role in the profession.

I

AN OVERVIEW OF LIBRARY INSTRUCTION

HISTORY AND BACKGROUND

"Library instruction" as we think of it today, refers to the use of buildings, locations, facilities, and materials in teaching users how to employ libraries to handle their information needs. In this broad sense, library instruction encompasses both "library orientation," the explanation of available library facilities and services, and "bibliographic instruction," the intensive process of teaching the efficient and effective use of the library by demonstrating library research methodology, search strategy, and the bibliographic structure of a given literature in a discipline. Library instruction can be an ad hoc on-the-spot incident, it can be an organized session explaining how certain bibliographical tools in a particular subject area are used, or it can be a highly structured formal program involving printed guides, slide/tapes, lecture sessions, and credit courses. Some illustrations of this process are as follows:

A public library, in cooperation with a school system, installs small computers to be used by children; the computers are connected to the library's holdings and the children learn how to call up books by author and title as part of a computer game. This is library instruction.

College juniors have to write research papers for their sociology class; they come to the library for a series of talks by the librarian on appropriate reference tools, books, articles, and pamphlets. This is library instruction.

An elementary school class of third graders is working on a play and wants authentic costumes and stage backgrounds. The school media center specialist helps them find the information they need through use of the card catalog and periodical indexes. This is library instruction.

A surgeon calls the medical library for immediate help in performing an unusual operation that only one or two doctors have done before. The librarian retrieves a pertinent article and puts the surgeon in touch with one of the doctors who performed the operation. This is library instruction.

An old man wants to find out how to make his pension money go farther in buying groceries. He reads a series of pamphlets on consumer education organized by the public library. This is library instruction.

Graduate students in chemistry need to know how certain new chemicals in the laboratory will react if combined. A call to the online data base searcher gives them several items, which they look up and read after some instruction in locating them is given by the librarian. This is library instruction.

Ninth graders in high school are working on a unit in English. They are reading *Romeo and Juliet* and viewing the film version of the play. The teacher and the librarian plan a unit together on the differences between film and print, using Shakespeare as a focus. This is library instruction.

The newspaper library maintains files of materials on local citizens for reference by community users. The librarian instructs the users on the unique way this "morgue" library is arranged. This is library instruction.

The idea of library instruction began to develop in the first half of the nineteenth century when librarians were generalists in education and acted as teachers by giving patrons instruction in use of libraries. Ralph Waldo Emerson, in 1858, called for a "professor of books," an instructor in library matters, and some years later Justin Winsor, at Harvard College, delivered lectures on library use as a librarian. This trend of having a "professor of books" was short-lived. The Civil War changed both lives and libraries, as did industrialization and the forging of mass society. Out of the cauldron of change came the secularization of knowledge, the increasing development of technology, and its focus on scientific research. These transformations led to changes within libraries. Up until the 1870s most education was broadly based. In the 1870s assistance to the reader, or reference service, came into being. Higher education began to focus on narrow subject disciplines rather than on general, broad-based knowledge.

At the same time that the reference desk was initiated by Samuel Green in the public library, Melvil Dewey founded his school of library economy. With these two events, technical training for librarians was emphasized, and there began a shift in library services away from research methods and towards bibliographical control. One sign of specialization was the development of vocational education programs that competed with the more traditional liberal arts courses of study. Up until the late 1870s the idea that librarians were educators or teachers had been affirmed by such people as Daniel Gilman, the president and librarian of Johns Hopkins University. Gilman's idea of a community of scholars influenced Johns Hopkins for decades. Azariah Root developed a practical program of user education at Oberlin College, and taught these principles to library science students at Case Western Reserve University. Root was one of the first librarians to combine practice with theory in library instruction.

With the new emphasis on technical aspects of libraries, other signs reflecting the new specialization appeared: elective course programs, credit units, and courses in library instruction. Even during the period between 1876 and 1910 there was an undercurrent of interest in user education. Some twenty institutions gave credit courses in library research and forty offered non-credit courses in library use.

In the 1920s and 1930s there were numerous efforts to establish library instruction programs, the most remarkable being the library-college movement developed by Louis Shores. This was to be a systematic, ideal way of instructing students in using libraries by having the library be the center of the college, and at the same time, its classroom. Students were to pursue information on their own in this new configuration, turning to each other as peers in the teaching process. When they could no longer find answers by themselves, students would call on the faculty to give them assistance. The faculty would then be expected to present lectures on the appropriate topics in the library. The library-college idea was based on independent study, and the faculty were librarian-teachers.

B. Lamar Johnson, of Stephens College, instituted a program at that institution which was actually realized and practiced for a number of years. Johnson was first and foremost an educator, the dean of instruction, who became a librarian in order to establish the program at Stephens. He wanted to make the curriculum and the library relevant to the lives of students. Johnson and his library staff worked closely with the faculty and students, instituted dormitory and division libraries, and initiated personal libraries for students. Students kept "reading diaries" of both personal and course-related reading. Several components of library instruction were well developed at Stephens: orientation, instruction in basic reference tools, interpretation and evaluation of library materials, and understanding of library materials. Point-of-use, individualized instruction, course-related and course-integrated instruction were all present in the Stephens College program.

Another spokesman for the library instruction movement was Harvie Branscomb, who studied the academic library in terms of its educational effectiveness. Branscomb believed that recreational reading was as important as educational reading, and he promoted dormitory libraries, exhibits, and topical lectures of interest to students. Most students, he felt, were unable to do research in libraries, and he proposed the use of faculty-library committees in which faculty and librarians would work together on developing effective programs for students. Branscomb rethought the roles of both faculty and librarians; both, he thought, should be available to students outside their normal workspaces — the library and the classroom. Librarians should be outside the library and attending classes, working with faculty and performing services in all kinds of ways; faculty, in his scheme, should come to the library and be available to students there.

During the 1940s and 1950s other attempts were made to institute library instruction programs. However, it was not until 1960, under the direction of Patricia Knapp at Monteith College in Wayne State University, that the concept of the library as the center of the learning process began to be articulated. Knapp wanted students to develop both a sophisticated understanding of the library and increased competency in its use. She felt that students should have library experiences which were closely related to their course work. This approach called for establishing new organizational structures for the library and new relationships between the librarians and faculty. Knapp was fortunate in her choice of Monteith; an inner-city college, it was composed of five hundred students and twenty faculty members. One of eleven liberal arts colleges in the university, it was fairly independent, with its own budget and administrative structure. Monteith was trying to approximate the kind of collegial atmosphere most likely to be found in the English universities, where students mingle with faculty in the common rooms.

When Knapp began her project, she chose her library assistants carefully and paid particular attention to qualities she felt would help them work effectively with classroom faculty. The Monteith College Library Experiment lasted only two years, ending before the results were achieved. Nevertheless, some sequences were developed which many library instruction librarians continue to use today: locating call numbers and the corresponding books for particular courses; locating information on specific topics while keeping a log or diary of the steps followed; writing a bibliographical essay; locating references on a revolutionary, social, religious, political, or artistic movement; locating information on one of several themes such as social mobility and its relationship to its social organization; locating information on the social and intellectual milieu of an artist; and identifying fifteen broad areas in the philosophy of science. Other assignments included an annotated bibliography on a particular topic, and an overview of the major sources, both in books and journal articles, that a nonspecialist could use. This latter assignment, used by instruction librarians as the "search strategy," was called "the path" or "the way" by Knapp. The library assignments were closely related to the academic classroom curriculum and to the teaching methods used by the academic classroom faculty at Monteith. The library sequences were designed to have unity, coherence, intellectual content, and practicality. Knapp's intention was to demonstrate to the faculty that the library was useful to them for teaching and doing research. The significance of the Monteith College Library Experiment was that for the first time the bibliographic structure of a discipline within the curriculum was tied to the library in an intellectual and theoretical framework by using practical library assignments. As a result of this project, many institutions had a blueprint to follow and librarians had examples and materials which they could adapt or adjust to suit their own situations at their institutions.

Just as the Civil War had done much to change lives and libraries, so did the war in Vietnam during the 1960s and its accompanying turbulent social changes. During this period libraries as institutions came under attack along with other cultural and educational establishments; they had always been repositories of culture and molders of civilization, but now they were being asked to become educational and social service institutions as well, to be all things to all users. Rapid technological changes were having a drastic impact on library services.

The academic ferment of the 1960s, with students desiring a more central role in their educational careers, provided further impetus to library instruction and helped shape the library instruction movement of the 1970s and 1980s. Along with active participation in the governance structures of higher education, students wanted to play an important part in shaping their own curriculum, including matriculation standards. Relevance was a key concept for these students of the 1960s, and one way of making libraries relevant to them was to ensure that they could use libraries effectively and efficiently. Students wanted no barriers when they looked for information; they wanted libraries to change in response to their immediate needs.

Most librarians were unable to meet these needs since they were equipped with neither the theoretical nor the practical knowledge necessary for effective library instruction. Most had never taught before. What they did have was a catalog of many methods and techniques that had been in the profession for generations, such as the reference interview, the tour, and the library lecture.

Most librarians felt competent and comfortable with these techniques since they were traditional ones and considered effective, but with the increased demand for relevance on the part of library users and a heavier use of library services, these methods became less workable and new ones had to be found. New methods and techniques were borrowed from other fields, or were originated by enterprising and creative librarians. But little thought was given to individual learning styles of users or techniques that were best suited to convey different types of information or teach different groups of users. One method or one technique was used for all users and all types of library instruction.

Essentially, the period of the 1960s was one of discontent; but for many librarians, it was a period of excitement and challenge as well. They began to experiment with other means, configurations, and formats. Soon groups of librarians were talking and writing about these various approaches and constructing guidelines and model statements for other librarians to follow. However, for some, these guidelines and model statements were too complex and elaborate and didn't apply to their own situations. There was still lacking a sound, practical approach that librarians could use and find workable.

As we have seen, librarians had already been agents of change, moving from their role as caretakers, conservators, custodians, and keepers of books to that of mediator, negotiation facilitator, and educator. However, as a result of the ferment of the 1960s, librarians have been challenged to become active in teaching the ways of the library to users. Consequently, library instruction, the process of teaching users to locate and evaluate information effectively and efficiently, has become a regular part of most services offered by libraries, along with circulation, reference, and interlibrary loan. Job descriptions for most public services listings that have been posted for all types of libraries now include phrases such as: "interest in educating library users desired," "must actively promote the use of the library," "ability to work with teachers in planning library assignments essential," "extensive faculty contact for orientation to the library necessary," "bibliographic instruction experience required," "implementation of library instruction program will be part of duties," and "interest in library user programs essential for the job."

SCHOOL, PUBLIC, AND SPECIAL LIBRARIES

Although the current library instruction movement has received the most attention and visibility in academic libraries, library instruction has occurred and continues to take place in school, public, and special libraries. The library instruction activities and programs are shaped by the library environment.

During the 1960s and 1970s, school libraries were planned to be part of the curriculum, with library skills integrated into each grade at varying levels. School librarians, or library media specialists, worked closely with teachers in developing lesson plans and class activities. Teachers viewed librarians as colleagues with expertise. Libraries were stressed as teaching units in most schools, particularly since the curriculum was mandated at state or district levels. Content and problem-solving skills were appropriate for library instruction activities, and students often created their own bibliographies, search strategies, and even their own readers' guides about particular subjects. Because school libraries have been a natural part of the educational process for students over many years, students are allowed to develop library skills which are built on graduated levels, the library instruction became systematic as it was integrated with classroom teaching. The Calgary Board of Education sequence of library research skills lists some 144 skills that students are expected to master from kindergarten through the twelfth grade. The New York State Bureau of School Libraries in its library media skills curriculum for elementary schools (K-6) lists individual skills for each grade level and for each subject that are to be mastered sequentially. Library skills instruction for schools follows the pattern for most programs: assessing needs; developing goals and objectives; modelling good search strategies; implementing the instruction; and evaluating the student's achievement in library skills instruction. Activity-centered learning has been popular in school media centers as a method of reinforcing learning and making the library instruction attractive. Games, puppets, plays, treasure hunts, and charades are just some of the techniques that have been used to encourage students to become involved in library instruction.

Unfortunately, budget cuts and decreasing school enrollments have curtailed many library instruction programs in the schools, and many school libraries have been forced to close or limit their activities. Competency-based education and curriculum mapping, two ideas which incorporated library skills for school children, are now uncommon in the schools. The 1980s will be a time of evaluating the educational priorities of the 1960s and 1970s, and library skills may not be one of them.

Public libraries have also been involved in library instruction, but with a different focus than the integrated model of school libraries. Public libraries have long had the mission of serving as repositories for history, literature, and the arts and providing information and reading materials for adults. The trends in the past ten or more years have been focused on vocational education, the independent learner, and career counseling. Public libraries have traditionally been places where adults could learn, but now the learning is tied in with job skills and job information centers. The reader advisory services of the 1930s and 1940s were the forerunners of the library instruction programs in the public libraries of the 1960s and 1970s. Book talks have given way to teaching users how to find the information they want, as recreational reading has been supplanted by consumer and employment needs.

Public libraries are particularly responsive to community needs, and programs for users are important for bringing clients to the library. Some public libraries offer library research skills courses, very much like the ones taught in colleges and universities. Others offer regular subject courses or specialized classes in great books, genealogy, or local history. Public libraries often attract their patrons through audiovisual means; videotaping, recording, and photographic possibilities for users have been included as part of general library instruction programs. Public libraries may become advocates for particular groups, and the library instruction can take the form of special activities, such as adult literacy programs or consumer awareness courses. The techniques used in school and academic libraries are also used by public libraries in their attempt to teach users how to find information.

Special libraries tend to have sophisticated users in that they, the users, know exactly what it is they want. Most special libraries are highly individualistic, usually devoted to a specific subject or area, such as medicine, pharmacy, electronics, engineering, or law. Special libraries have predominated in the sciences, where currency and immediacy of information are important. Library instruction in special libraries follows the same principles as for other libraries, but the focus may be narrower, both for the users and the topics. In special libraries, either the collection is of a restricted nature or the library serves a well-defined body of users with a staff trained in a particular area or method, offering personalized services. The special librarian often goes to the office or laboratory of the users, rather than waiting for users to come to the library, so library instruction and service are active rather than passive. Special libraries may use different forms for their materials—computers, data bases, audiotapes, and films may make up the library collection rather than books and periodicals. In most special libraries speed is usually important, since the users are often engaged in life-saving research or in competitive business. Special libraries tend to be smaller than most public or academic libraries, although many large libraries have special libraries or collections within them. The objectives are focused directly on the information needs of the users, and this provides a framework for the special library which lends itself to change.

Library instruction programs have similar goals in whatever type of libraries they occur. Instruction librarians share mutual concerns and common efforts in trying to meet the same ends—to get users to locate information efficiently and effectively—and they use the same skills to accomplish their goals; in one case it may mean teaching particular tools or skills and in another it may mean instructing patrons in how to approach a certain discipline of literature. Libraries in the 1980s are reexamining and reevaluating their programs. As users change and seek new ways to learn about the world and locate information, libraries will have to change in order to meet users' needs. Instruction librarians in academic, school, public, and special libraries can all learn from each other and try out the various methods and techniques that have been developed. Adult learning, lifelong learning, and continuing education are a part of all libraries, and instruction librarians can identify with each other without necessarily being involved in the same type of library.

ORGANIZATIONS AND CLEARINGHOUSES

There are numerous organizations actively engaged in all aspects of library instruction, and new ones are being formed all the time. The American Library Association has five such organizations within its own structure. The Instruction in the Use of Libraries Committee, the first to be organized, covers all libraries. Appendix A gives a broad library statement.

The Association of College and Research Libraries fostered the library instruction movement with its Bibliographic Instruction Task Force, which began in 1971 and developed several significant documents. Appendices B and C are two of the documents. The Task Force attracted many interested librarians to its meetings, and in 1977 ACRL formed the Bibliographic Instruction Section (BIS) to continue the work of the Task Force. BIS is one of the larger sections within ACRL and numbers close to 3,000 members. BIS has been active in publishing documents: a bibliographic instruction handbook, a directory of clearinghouses, a set of checklists for model library instruction programs, and guidelines for evaluation have been produced by this group. The section has also been active in presenting conferences and programs on library instruction at ALA conferences.

Simultaneously with the formation of the BIS section, ALA also began a library instruction roundtable for all types of libraries. The Library Instruction Round Table (LIRT) draws together many school, public, and special librarians as well as academic librarians. ALA's policy statement on instruction in the use of libraries appears in Appendix A of this text. ACRL has two other organizations which are also involved with library instruction, the Committee on Bibliographic Instruction for Educators within the Education and Behavioral Science Section, and the Instruction and Use Committee within the Junior College Section.

The most prominent national organization aside from the national ALA groups for library instruction is the Library Orientation Instruction Exchange (LOEX) at the Center for Educational Resources at Eastern Michigan University in Ypsilanti, Michigan. Funded initially by the Council on Library Resources in 1971, LOEX has become a national depository and clearinghouse for instructional materials. Sample materials are collected, arranged, and loaned to librarians who call, write, or visit for information on particular library instruction programs. LOEX also produces its own newsletter, *LOEX News*, a quarterly containing items of interest in the field such as recent publications, programs, or upcoming library instruction conferences, as well as reports on past conferences. LOEX encourages the grass roots support of library instruction through its activities. It hosts an annual conference each May for several days of talks, presentations, discussions, and participation in all areas of library instruction for all types of libraries. Academic, school, public, and special librarians, along with faculty members, administrators, and teachers, have attended these meetings.

The papers from the conference, published each year by Pierian Press in Ann Arbor, Michigan, constitute the major writings of the 1970's library instruction movement. LOEX has been a major force in the library instruction movement, the instigating and inspirational power for many librarians just beginning library instruction activities. As Evan Farber, a leader in the instruction movement, noted about one of the LOEX conferences:

> ... This conference was not designed primarily for the benefit of those, like myself, who have practiced, thought about, and discussed library instruction for a long time. Rather, it is for the many persons here who perhaps don't have colleagues who are eager or even willing to talk about library instruction. For them, these few days serve as—if not spiritual renewal—certainly professional reinforcement and encouragement, and they have the chance to learn again that they are not alone, that there are other librarians who share their philosophy and objectives, their plans and frustrations, and that there are programs that are well on their way which can offer counsel and inspiration.[1]

Other national clearinghouses include Great Britain's national library instruction clearinghouse, the Library Instruction Materials Bank (LIMB) and the Information Officer for User Education at Loughborough University of Technology in Loughborough, Leicestershire, England. Australia also has a national clearinghouse, the Data Bank for User Education Materials with the Chief Librarian at the Cauldfield Institute of Technology at Victoria, Australia.

---

[1]Evan Farber in *Faculty Involvement in Library Instruction*. Library Orientation Services. Papers presented at the annual LOEX conferences. Ann Arbor, MI: Pierian Press, 1976, p. 105.

Aside from national activity, there is a great deal of interest in, and attention paid to, library instruction on the regional and state levels. Conferences and workshops on library instruction are held in many regions and various states, including: South Carolina, Florida, California, Pennsylvania, and Washington, DC. The proceedings are often published, adding to the literature about library instruction. Regional clearinghouses exist in New England and the Southeast. There are currently state clearinghouses for many states, including: Arizona, California, Florida, Hawaii, Indiana, Kansas, Kentucky, Maine, New Jersey, and New York. Many are organized separately, and some are part of the state library associations for librarians. A few specialized clearinghouses, established by subject area or by type of library, exist: art libraries, theological libraries, and secondary school libraries all have their own clearinghouses. Most clearinghouses either publish their own newsletters, have regular columns in library journals, or contribute news items to other library publications. Many sponsor workshops and conferences or act as informal consultants to members who have problems with library instruction. Clearinghouses in library instruction are excellent sources of information and expertise on the local level for librarians interested in library instruction.

THE LITERATURE AND STATE OF THE ART

Most of the writings about library instruction in the twentieth century have been in the form of journal articles or papers from instruction conferences. There is just beginning to exist a canon or collection of literature in library instruction which is more than listings of descriptions and details of library instruction programs at various individual institutions. Several model statements and guidelines have appeared as the production of concerned librarians working through state and national professional organizations.

With the organization of many clearinghouses, information about library instruction programs began to be pooled. Whereas the clearinghouses provide models by means of actual samples, and psychological support through personal contacts, the literature attempts to provide theoretical background to the materials.

Historically, library instruction draws from a rich heritage of literature from earlier periods. The works of B. Lamar Johnson, Louis Shores, and Harvie Branscomb can still be read with profit for defining and understanding many of the concepts upon which library instruction rests. The library-college movement of the 1930s, with its proposal that small clusters of students work individually with faculty tutors in the library, advocated well-developed library skills. Although this movement never gained widespread acceptance, Patricia Knapp and her program at Wayne State University in Monteith College built on the library-college idea, and spurred a new wave of interest in library skills and library instruction. Knapp's work was not completed, but it did provide an impetus for further work in the field of library instruction. The best-known program of the 1960s that is still in existence is the one at Earlham College in Richmond, Indiana, described at length by Evan Farber, James Kennedy, and Thomas Kirk.

In the 1970s the literature of library instruction began to expand rapidly. The LOEX conference series, published by Pierian Press, began in 1971 and has produced articles and papers covering the various aspects of the library instruction movement. *Reference Services Review*, which started in 1974, has an annual annotated review of the literature for library instruction. Little monographic literature exists aside from the LOEX series. John Lubans edited two compilations of articles in *Educating the Library User* in 1974, and *Progress in Educating the Library Users* in 1978. Deborah Lockwood's bibliography, *Library Instruction*, in 1979, and Beverly Renford and Linnea Hendrickson's handbook, *Bibliographic Instruction*, in 1980, are other contributions to the literature of library instruction.

Most of the literature for library instruction has been in the form of articles and can be retrieved by using the following indexes: *Library Literature, Education Index*, and *Resources in Education*. While there has been an inordinate amount of literature about library instruction, little of it rests on solid research. Most articles describe particular programs in library instruction, and are of the "how we do it here" type. Noticeably lacking are such elements of good research as: the problem defined, the hypothesis stated, the research design given, the methodology used, the evaluation tried, or conclusion from the process.

Many reasons have been cited in the literature for the proliferation and acceptance of library instruction programs in addition to the historical antecedents. The enthusiasm and energy of instruction librarians in the 1970s were infectious, and they wrote about and discussed their ideas and programs among themselves in the journal literature and at library instruction conferences. Workshops and seminars devoted to various aspects of library instruction became popular, with their growth increasing markedly in the 1970s. These were offered by national and state associations, local consortia, individual libraries, interested librarians, and library schools in their continuing education programs. The workshops and seminars dealt not only with planning and designing instruction programs, preparing and evaluating materials, teaching and running programs, but leading and administering them as well.

Grant monies from national and state sources particularly geared towards library instruction programs became available in the 1970s. For example, the Council on Library Resources and the National Endowment for the Humanities gave large amounts of money in their Enhancement Program. These grants enabled those few libraries to plan and implement library instruction programs that otherwise might not have been developed, and provided visibility and credibility to those programs, a development that was important politically for library instruction. Most good instruction programs have succeeded, not always because of grant monies but because they are well-thought-out and well-planned programs with strong collegial and administrative backing. Other library instruction programs have ended with the funding. The National Endowment for the Humanities continues to give support to libraries for public programming involving the humanities with the community, and opportunities for library instruction programs exist within that framework.

The current status of library instruction parallels the literature; there are all types of programs and activities, but few that have held up over time and that are well integrated into their institutions. Many methods are being used to provide tours and orientation, to teach basic library skills, and to instruct on the higher research level within the disciplines. Also, there are independent learning programs, ranging from self-instructional printed packages and workbooks to slide/tapes and automated computer-assisted instruction. Course-related, course-integrated, point-of-use, and programmed methods are all employed as librarians attempt to teach library instruction skills in various ways. The range of possibilities for planning and implementing library instruction programs is a wide one.

Libraries traditionally have been organized and structured to acquire, catalog, store, and preserve materials, and the departments of acquisitions, cataloging, circulation, and reference have been developed and maintained to reflect that organization and structure. But the emphasis over the last ten years has shifted from collecting and storing library materials to using and understanding library materials. The focus is on library users and their informational needs rather than on materials and their bibliographical control. Users come to libraries to get library materials, to verify that particular works exist, to obtain answers to specific questions, to study in the library, and to receive instruction in using library services and materials. The traditional organizational structures of libraries that were established to emphasize the collecting and processing of materials are not appropriate for educating users in the service functions. This dichotomy between the structure of the organization and the function it performs has made it more difficult for library instruction programs to establish themselves since there is not a natural fit between the library instruction practices and the traditional departments of most libraries. The administrative and technical aspects of the hierarchical structures of libraries have tended to dominate the academic ones.

Libraries are complex institutions. This complexity is taken for granted by most librarians working within the professions, but for users libraries are confusing and can be frustrating. The bureaucratic organizational structure of the institution adds to this confusion and frustration. Users don't care about the categories of library staff (librarians, nonprofessionals, paraprofessionals, clerks, or secretaries); the bibliographic apparatus of books, magazines, and documents (Library of Congress, Dewey Decimal, KWIC, or SuDoc); or the technological interventions in using computers to access information (BRS, LCS, MEDLARS, DIALOG, INFORM, or OCLC). They want answers to their questions or help in finding them, but the structure within libraries works against providing the very assistance libraries strive for.

The differences between the philosophies of librarianship taught by library school faculty and practiced by librarians, especially in the area of public services and reference services, are noteworthy. Library school faculty argue that research and theory should be the chief matters of concern for library school students since practices change so quickly. Practicing librarians suggest that skills and practices may be as important as theories and ideas. Most library school faculty are not intimately acquainted with the daily situations that arise in real libraries; consequently, the skills and techniques that librarians need for communicating, interviewing, supervising, and teaching may be lacking from most library school courses.

Reference librarians face library users on a daily basis and know their behavior through realistic, tangible, practical experiences and observations. Library school faculty who teach reference courses to future reference librarians, on the other hand, may not have worked at a reference desk; rather, their expertise may come from the practicing librarians they know, the students they teach, or the reading they do. In addition, the theoreticians who teach and the practitioners who work may not belong to the same professional organizations within the American Library Association, their national association.

This division between theory and practice is not unique to the library profession. Law, medicine, and nursing maintain both clinical and academic approaches in their professions. But, because of this division, the teaching and the practicing of librarianship may differ markedly, particularly in the area of public services. Many library school faculty advocate the role of librarian as provider of information rather than educator. Providers tell users what they need to have in terms of their wants and supply it for them; educators teach users to ask the proper questions and train them to discover and evaluate their sources. In short, some library school faculty, without having worked in libraries themselves, are teaching students to be librarians, and are apt to view library instruction as part of reference, rather than reference as part of library instruction.

The work style and the mission of library instruction are at odds with the hierarchical bureaucracy of libraries and the outlook of most professional schools of librarianship. The library instruction movement is trying to reshape and redefine librarianship. This view of librarianship is attempting to instill a new paradigm since new thinking is needed. Because it focuses on users and their needs, in a "holistic" sense, users develop personal responsibility for finding information in libraries.

SUGGESTED READINGS

Anderson, Pauline, "What's Going on in Independent Schools?" *School Library Journal* 26 (November 1979): 33-41.

Association of College and Research Libraries, Bibliographic Instruction Section, Policy and Planning Committee. *Bibliographic Instruction Handbook*. Chicago, IL: American Library Association, 1979.

Bell, Irene Wood, and Jeanne E. Wieckert. *Basic Media Skills through Games*. Littleton, CO: Libraries Unlimited, 1979.

Biggs, Mary. "A Proposal for Course-Related Library Instruction." *School Library Journal* 26 (January 1980): 34-37.

Blazek, Ronald. *Influencing Students toward Media Center Use*. Chicago, IL: American Library Association, 1975.

Bowers, Melvyn K. *Library Instruction in the Elementary School*. Metuchen, NJ: Scarecrow, 1971.

Branscomb, Harvie. *Teaching with Books: A Study of College Libraries*. Chicago, IL: American Library Association, 1940.

Calgary Board of Education, Canada. *Research Skills: A Scope and Sequence Chart of Library and Information Skills*. Calgary, Canada: Board of Education, 1976.

Cammack, Floyd M.; Marri DeCasin; and Norman Roberts. *Community College Library Instruction: Training for Self-Reliance in Basic Library Use*. Hamden, CT: Shoe String Press, 1979.

Childers, Thomas. "Trends in Public Library I & R Services." *Library Journal* 104 (October 1, 1979): 2035-39.

Davies, Ruth Ann. *The School Library Media Center: A Force for Educational Excellence*. New York: Bowker, 1979.

Drake, Miriam A. "The Management of Libraries as Professional Organizations." *Special Libraries* 68 (May/June 1977): 181-86.

Fjallbrant, Nancy, and Malcolm B. Stevenson. *User Education in Libraries.* Hamden, CT: Linnet Books, 1978.

Flexner, Jennie. *Making Books Work.* New York: Simon & Schuster, 1943.

Frey, Amy Louise, and Saul Spigel. "Educating Adult Users in the Public Library." *Library Journal* 104 (April 15, 1979): 895-96.

Galloway, Sue. "Nobody Is Teaching the Teachers." *Booklegger* 3 (January 1976): 29-31.

Hart, Thomas. *Instruction in School Media Center Use.* Chicago, IL: American Library Association, 1978.

Hogan, Sharon Anne. "Training and Education of Library Instruction Librarians." *Library Trends* 29 (Summer 1980): 105-126.

Hopkins, Frances L. "User Instruction in the College Library: Origins, Prospects, and a Practical Program." In *College Librarianship*, edited by William Miller and D. Stephen Rockwood, pp. 173-204. Metuchen, NJ: Scarecrow, 1981.

Johnson, B. Lamar. *The Librarian and the Teacher in General Education: A Report of Library-Instructional Activities at Stephens College.* Chicago, IL: American Library Association, 1948.

Johnson, B. Lamar. *Vitalizing a College Library.* Chicago, IL: American Library Association, 1939.

Kenney, Donald J. "Universal Library Skills: An Outdated Concept." *Southeastern Librarian* 1 (Spring 1980): 13-14.

Kirk, Thomas G. "Past, Present and Future of Library Instruction." *The Southeastern Librarian* 27 (Spring 1977): 15-18.

Kirk, Thomas G., and Mary Jo Lynch. "Bibliographic Instruction in Academic Libraries: New Developments." *Drexel Library Quarterly* 8 (July 1972): 357-65.

Kirkendall, Carolyn A. "Cooperation, Coordination and Communication: The LOEX Clearinghouse Experience." In *Library User Education: Are New Approaches Needed?*, edited by Peter K. Fox, Report No. 5503. London: British Library, 1980.

Kirkendall, Carolyn A. "Library Use Education: Current Practices and Trends." *Library Trends* 29 (Summer 1980): 29-37.

Knapp, Patricia B. *The Monteith College Library Experiment.* Metuchen, NJ: Scarecrow Press, 1966.

Library Orientation Series: Papers Presented at the Annual LOEX Conferences. Ann Arbor, MI: Pierian Press, 1972-1981.
Library Orientation, 1972.
A Challenge for Academic Libraries, 1973.
Planning and Developing a Library Orientation Program, 1975.

Evaluating Library Use Instruction, 1975.

Academic Library Instruction; Objectives, Programs, and Faculty Involvement, 1975.

Faculty Involvement in Library Instruction, 1976.

Library Instruction in the Seventies: State of the Art, 1977.

Putting Instruction in Its Place: In the Library and in the Library School, 1978.

Improving Library Instruction; How to Teach and How to Evaluate, 1979.

Directions for the Decade: Library Instruction in the 1980's, 1980.

Teaching Library Use Competence: Bridging the Gap between High School and College, 1981.

Lockwood, Deborah L. *Library Instruction: A Bibliography*. Westport, CT: Greenwood Press, 1979.

Lubans, John. *Educating the Library User*. New York: Bowker, 1974.

Lubans, John. *Progress in Educating the Library User*. New York: Bowker, 1978.

Margrabe, Mary. "The Library Media Specialist and Total Curriculum Involvement." *Catholic Library World* 49 (February 1978): 283-87.

Melum, Verna V. "1971 Survey of Library Orientation and Instruction Programs." *Drexel Library Quarterly* 7 (July-October 1971): 225-53.

Miller, Edward P. "User-Oriented Planning." *Special Libraries* 64 (November 1973): 479-82.

Monroe, Margaret E. *Library Adult Education*. New York: Scarecrow Press, 1963.

Nordling, Jo Anne. *Dear Faculty: A Discovery Method Guide Book to the High School Library*. Westwood, MA: Faxon Co., 1976.

Penland, Patrick R., and Aleyamma Mathal. *The Library as a Learning Service Center*. New York: Dekker, 1978.

Renford, Beverly, and Linnea Hendrickson. *Bibliographic Instruction: A Handbook*. New York: Neal-Schuman Publishers, 1980.

Rice, A. Carolyn. "The Tyranny of 'the Bells: Reflections on the Difference between School and Public Librarianship." *Library Journal* 103 (March 15, 1978): 618-20.

Robertson, W. Davenport. "A User-Oriented Approach to Setting Priorities for Library Services." *Special Libraries* 71 (August 1980): 345-53.

Shapiro, Lillian L. *Teaching Yourself in Libraries: A Guide to the High School Media Center and Other Libraries*. New York: Wilson, 1978.

Shores, Louis. *The Generic Book: What It Is and How It Works*. Norman, OK: Library College Associates, 1977.

Shores, Louis. *Library-College USA: Essays on a Prototype for an American Higher Education*. Tallahassee, FL: South Pass Press, 1970.

Smith, Helen Lyman. *Adult Education Activities in Public Libraries.* Chicago, IL: American Library Association, 1954.

Strable, Edward G. *Special Libraries: A Guide for Management.* New York: Special Libraries Association, 1975.

Trinkner, Charles L. *Teaching for Better Use of Libraries.* Hamden, CT: Shoe String Press, 1970.

Tucker, John Mark. "The Origins of Bibliographic Instruction in Academic Libraries, 1876-1914." In *New Horizons for Academic Libraries*, edited by Robert Stueart and Richard D. Johnson, pp. 268-76. New York: K. G. Saur, 1979.

Tucker, John Mark. "User Education in Academic Libraries: A Century in Retrospect." *Library Trends* 29 (Summer 1980): 9-27.

University of the State of New York, The State Education Department. *The Elementary Library Media Skills Curriculum.* Albany, NY: Bureau of School Libraries, The State Education Department, 1980.

Walker, A. Thomas, and Paula K. Montgomery. *Teaching Media Skills: An Instructional Program for Elementary and Middle School Students.* Littleton, CO: Libraries Unlimited, 1977.

Waltzer, Margaret A. "Library Instruction in Secondary Schools." *Catholic Library World* 48 (April 1977): 402-403.

Wehmeyer, Lillian Biermann. *The School Librarian as Educator.* Littleton, CO: Libraries Unlimited, 1976.

Wittkopf, Barbara J. *Library Instruction Clearinghouses: 1981, A Directory.* Chicago, IL: American Library Association, ACRL, BIS, Committee on Cooperation, Clearinghouse Subcommittee, 1981.

II

IMPLEMENTING THE PROGRAM

ORIENTATION: THE FIRST STEP

In library instruction, orientation means becoming acquainted with the physical aspects of the library and becoming aware of library services and materials. Like travellers in foreign countries, users need to get their bearings with basic information on the library: where it is located, what hours it is open, how it is laid out, and what it offers. Orientation is the beginning basic step in any library instruction program since users must know how the library is arranged physically before they can proceed further in gathering information. If libraries do nothing else, they usually offer some kind of orientation, whether by a printed self-guided tour, a map, an audiovisual presentation, or an informal chat or walking tour with one of the library staff members. Figure 1 (see p. 34) is a sample of a self-guided tour.

The physical environment of a facility is important to most people; it can affect their social and intellectual attitudes and behaviors. Light, heat, and furniture are all important factors in library surroundings. Libraries can be confusing places to users because of the complex arrangement of materials. If the surroundings are pleasant, and if users know their way around libraries physically, they are more comfortable, and their frustrations and anxieties can be reduced. The books don't look so forbidding in the stacks, and the imposing library buildings appear less formidable.

There are many methods of conducting orientation in libraries. The informal tour by library staff members is traditional and very effective. Users have a personal escort who can answer their questions, and the tour can be shaped to the particular interests of the group or individual. Some drawbacks to this way of providing orientation are that it can be very time-consuming for staff, some staff members may be better at it than others, inconsistencies may arise in the information that is conveyed, and it may not always be possible to provide this personal guided tour when users want or need it.

Audiovisual methods that have been developed and used by many libraries for orientation purposes are popular, since the audiotape guided tour can be taken at the users' convenience and will contain consistent and uniform information. Some difficulties with using audiovisual methods may occur, however. Equipment is required for listening, so headphones and cassette players must be purchased, maintained, and repaired. In addition, the logistics of checking out the tapes and equipment may complicate library operations. The use of slide/tapes is another method that has been used effectively for orientation purposes. The slide/tapes can be shown to individuals or to groups, depending upon the available space. They can be used outside of the library and can be viewed many times if needed. Slide/tapes are relatively easy to update, but the same equipment problems of purchasing, maintaining, and repairing that applied to the audiotape method apply here as well. Scripts have to be written, slides taken and mounted, and revisions made. Some libraries use only slides; some only audiotapes.

By far the most common method for orienting users to libraries is printed materials. Maps, signs, handbooks, guides, and self-guided tours are all used for this basic level of library instruction. More and more libraries are taking cues from supermarkets and department stores and are labelling the areas of their buildings with graphics and signs. Printed self-guided tours have many advantages: they can be available at the time of the users' needs; they are relatively easy to produce; they can be used to provide other useful information about the library; they are good public relations tools for libraries; and they can be widely distributed.

Whatever method is used for this basic level of orientation, users should get a solid foundation in knowing the physical arrangement and services of libraries in the beginning of the library instruction program.

TEACHING AND LIBRARY INSTRUCTION

The knowledge explosion has produced so much information that bibliographic control has become cumbersome and confusing, especially in libraries. Library instruction is needed more than ever to interpret this disarray of information to users and to teach them how to find what they want. The human element is still one of the most important variables of all in effective teaching, and instruction librarians may have overlooked it in their enthusiasm to teach users about the library. Too often teaching "tools" such as workbooks, exercises, or audiovisual packages have been used in place of librarians. Instruction librarians need to use techniques that will not create another barrier between them and their users, which means that they must have a solid grounding in techniques and know which ones promote learning. Barriers exist within the library already: the classification schemes; the cataloging codes; the filing rules; the print and nonprint formats of information; the computer accessing systems; the interlibrary loan system; and the rules and regulations governing the use of the library. With the functions of the library evolving towards more sophisticated technology and networks, emphasis is shifting away from technical control and toward teaching users how to handle the networks and the technology in libraries. Instruction is one way, and often an indispensable one, to make all of this available to the users; without effective teaching techniques to educate users, libraries are in danger of creating barriers by the very wealth of services they offer.

Many educational theorists have elaborated on their views of teaching, and there is a consensus among them that more is known about learning than about teaching. Most teaching is based on memory, one of the weakest learning faculties, and one which can stifle learning. Some educators propose focusing more on processes by observing changes that occur in students during teaching sessions to see how learning occurs.

The teaching-learning process is a complex one. Questions educators ask about the process are:

1. What are the necessary conditions under which learning occurs?

2. What are the results in learning using repetitive practice, reward, punishment, or stimuli?

Learning is the acquisition of knowledge or skill or the process by which behavior changes as a result of experience. The teaching-learning process is important for instruction librarians; their view of the process determines which modes or methods to use in presenting their library instruction. A good learning experience includes several elements in the interaction: involvement, challenge, support, structure, feedback, application, and integration.

Two basic approaches to the teaching-learning process are the stimulus-response method and the cognitive method. The stimulus-response method promotes acquiring the appropriate learning by changing the environment in certain ways so that learning will occur. This method is based on repetition and reinforcement, and the users are active participants in the teaching-learning process. The cognitive method helps users develop insights into problems by employing examples and structures. This method is based on testing hypotheses and getting feedback from users; the users are active participants in the teaching-learning process using this method also. Instruction librarians are interested in knowing which circumstances are the most conducive for learning and which techniques are appropriate for different users and different situations.

The teaching-learning process ideally is one of resonance, where both teachers and learners are on the same wave length and the teaching process is at a level appropriate to the learning process. The timing of the instruction, the environment of the situation, and the amount and presentation of the information are all crucial factors in the teaching-learning process. Small amounts of information given frequently are usually best. Students are not apt to pay attention if the material is too difficult or too easy or if it consists of too much or too little substance.

The practical details of teaching are important to pay attention to in order to keep distractions from interrupting the teaching-learning process. Changing the order in presenting the materials, trying out new approaches or new methods, experimenting with different examples, or using aids such as audiovisual equipment, easels with newsprint, or blackboards are all ways of enhancing the teaching-learning process. The time of day, the day of week, even the month of the year, can affect the teaching situation. The location of the teaching area, whether it is a classroom or part of the library, its size, configuration, the arrangement of furniture within it, are all important details which can influence the teaching-learning process.

Personality and style also enter into the teaching-learning process, and it is necessary for instruction librarians to feel comfortable in their teaching to be successful. Formality or informality is a matter of taste. Teaching has been characterized as an art, a skill, a science, a social affair, and a performance. The two most common models that exist for teaching are the lecture and the discussion. Teachers using the first model take on roles of imparters or dispensers of knowledge; in the second model teachers are coaches or facilitators. In addition to basic competence and intelligence, effective teachers should possess such important attributes as compassion, enthusiasm, and humor. Criticism and praise are valuable to students, while expertise and encouragement are necessary for assisting them in learning new material. Teachers must be careful not to get in the way and obstruct the material being taught, and this is especially true for instruction librarians. Teachers need to be subject specialists, psychologists, and educators, all at the same time.

For teaching library skills, instruction librarians need to know where the students are in terms of their knowledge and expertise in library use. Facts should relate to each other and be organized in a meaningful fashion. Integrated knowledge and understanding of library use are primary goals, and a range of treatments for each topic at different levels is essential. Teaching experts suggest that it can be dysfunctional to begin any teaching-learning activity with rules and regulations, and that it is far better to start with relevant data and information. In this way students begin with a comfortable environment and are not apt to be threatened or antagonized. Observant teachers want to know when their students are saturated and when to stop, when to give diagnostic exercises, when to review or to change the pace. Instruction librarians should simply ask their users to tell them when the saturation point has been reached.

Most library schools do little, if any, preparation for teaching. Therefore, instruction librarians have tended to rely on their previous experiences as teachers, to set up some training programs with sympathetic colleagues, or, more often than not, to teach their library instruction skills in whatever fashion they could manage. Instruction librarians take courses in teaching methods, attend practical workshops on teaching techniques, or visit each other to observe teaching sessions of library instruction skills. If there are videotaping facilities available, videotaping library instruction sessions can be a useful way to analyze teaching techniques. If sympathetic colleagues are willing, they can be asked to observe library instruction sessions and critique the teaching techniques. Some common problems that instruction librarians seem to have with their teaching are: not looking at users or establishing eye contact; speaking too rapidly; giving out too much information at once; pausing infrequently to allow for questions; not involving the audience; not handling the aids well; not speaking loudly enough; making presentations ponderous; taking themselves too seriously and not allowing for levity and spontaneity. A checklist of guidelines for effective teaching techniques is shown in Figure 2 (see p. 37).

The teaching-learning process is an integral human activity that occurs daily. Instruction librarians can become skilled in this activity through practice and by working with colleagues in critiquing their teaching.

CONCEPTS AND STRUCTURES

Instruction librarians generally agree that some inaccuracies exist about library instruction research skills. One inaccuracy is that classroom faculty want to teach the content of a subject, while instruction librarians want to teach the structure of the subject. Instruction librarians argue that research skills are part of library instruction skills. The analysis of the research process has produced a body of literature which continues to be in the tradition of library instruction, consisting of studies about the analytical methods used by scholars in the social sciences and the humanities in gathering their data for research. Citation pattern studies exist for research done in the sciences. Library instruction, as a part of the discipline of library science, is more than just organizing the information and leading users to it.

Instruction librarians demonstrate that library research skills are more than technical skills and are linked to conceptual frameworks. Just as classroom teachers are said to teach content over process, so instruction librarians are said to teach location over use and evaluation. Since library skills are suitable for acquiring information, gaining knowledge, and applying this to unknown situations, it is important to outline the concepts of the skills and the constructions or frameworks to which they can be applied.

The idea of conceptual frameworks is not a new one for library instruction. Patricia Knapp in her Monteith College Library Experiment used them for the assignments in the library sequences she developed. The search strategy approach uses the idea of conceptual frameworks. What is novel is that instruction librarians are now consciously integrating their knowledge about the types of library materials or tools and the subject areas or disciplines into a teaching-learning process that will make it easier for users to understand and to remember the idea of linking content with process. Instruction librarians have learned by their experiences that it is important to connect a particular skill with a topic, or a subject with an acquired ability. In order to transfer this knowledge beyond its special situation it must be tied to a structure. An example is a search strategy on a current topic in political affairs when it might be important to be aware of the source of the document, i.e., is it a governmental agency, a news bureau, or an analyst?

Examples of other conceptual frameworks are: citations which can be studied in order to see how a key article builds on others and is also built on itself; the common occurrence of key works in numerous subject bibliographies of a field; the types of reference books in a specific discipline; the kind of format for a subject area, such as monographs, journals, or annual reviews; the types of sources in a particular discipline, such as primary or secondary; and the way information is disseminated or distributed, such as by conference papers, workshop talks, periodical or journal articles, books or monographs.

Figure 1
SAMPLE SELF-GUIDED TOUR

The university welcomes you to its library. This self-guided tour is designed for your independent orientation to our collections and services. The tour you are about to take is for the main library. The Downtown Campus Branch and the School of Library and Information Science Library are our two branch libraries.

The university library maintains an open stack policy which means you find your own books on the shelves. The collection contains nearly one million volumes of books and periodicals. The main collection is contained on four floors: reference, government documents, circulation are on the first floor; the circulating collection of books is on the second and third floors; and the basement level contains periodicals, microforms, reserve books, and the learning resources materials.

Figure 1 (cont'd)

STATION 1: Circulation Desk.
Begin here at the long desk which faces you as you enter the library. Library materials that you get may be charged out here and should be returned here as well. If you are unable to find the books you need, check here. You must have a valid identification card in order to check out books.

STATION 2: Reference Desk.
As you turn left from the circulation desk, you will face the reference area; the reference desk is the long desk in front of you. Librarians at this desk can answer your questions on the use of the card catalog or other library reference tools or services.

STATION 3: Location Directory.
Between the reference desk and the circulation desk is the location directory, which gives you the outline of the Library of Congress classification scheme and guides you to where these books are on the shelves in our library. The directory also explains prefixes used.

STATION 4: Card Catalog.
Behind the reference desk is the card catalog. It is divided into two sections: author/title and subject. If you have difficulty using the card catalog, consult with the reference librarians.

STATION 5: Reference Collection: Books.
As you leave the card catalog, turn right into the front wing of the library. Here is the reference book collection, including such items as encyclopedias, dictionaries, directories, guides, and atlases. Bibliographies are also included in this collection.

STATION 6: Abstracts and Indexes.
At the opposite end of the wing from the reference collection, on the other side of the card catalog, is the section containing the abstracts and indexes. There are general as well as subject abstracts and indexes.

STATION 7: Interlibrary Loan.
To the right of the abstracts and indexes area is the interlibrary loan office. If there is a book, journal article, or dissertation you need for your research that we do not own, you may borrow it from another library through this office.

STATION 8: Vertical File and Career File.
At the end of the abstracts and indexes area are the vertical file and career file. Both contain pamphlets arranged by subject or careers; material may be checked out at the circulation desk.

STATION 9: College Catalogs.
Just beyond the vertical file and career file area is a section devoted to college catalogs from all over the country and from foreign countries. They are arranged alphabetically by state or by country.

STATION 10: Information Retrieval.
Near the interlibrary loan office you will note the information retrieval office, which formulates computer-produced bibliographies for many data bases. Computer searches are available only by appointments, which can be made through this office.

(Figure 1 continues on page 36.)

Figure 1 (cont'd)

STATION 11: Government Documents.
Across the lobby from the reference desk is the government documents area, which contains material from the United States (counties, cities, and towns), as well as Great Britain and the United Nations.

Please proceed downstairs by the stairs on either side of the circulation desk to the basement level, where you may proceed with the library tour.

STATION 12: Periodicals Room.
Follow the signs to the periodicals room, where most of the periodicals are kept. Current displays of particular titles are separate from the bound journals in the stacks. This room has an information desk should you require any assistance in using this collection.

STATION 13: Microforms Room.
Opposite the periodicals room is the microforms room, which has many formats of library materials including books and periodicals on microform. Reading machines are available here for you to use.

STATION 14: Reserve Room.
Off the microforms room is the reserve room, where library materials are placed on reserve for class or special use. Materials are listed under the name of the faculty member placing them on reserve.

STATION 15: Learning Resources Center.
Opposite the reserve room is the learning resources center, which contains curriculum materials, audiovisual materials, and phonograph records. Machines and equipment for using these materials are also housed here, and assistance is available at the desk.

STATION 16: Special Collections.
Walk back through the microforms room towards the periodicals room. Just before entering the periodicals room you will notice a sign directing you to special collections on the left. Walk down this corridor and you will be in the area of special collections. This section contains material which requires special handling or is of a valuable nature. Rare books, manuscripts, reprint series, and specialized subject collections are located here.

STATION 17: University Archives.
Across from the special collections section is the university archives. Materials relating to the university and its history are located here. Official records, masters' theses, doctoral dissertations, and personal papers and publications of officers and faculty are housed here. Librarians are available to help you with both the special collections and the archive materials.

You have now reached the end of your tour. We hope you have enjoyed the self-guided tour of the library. Please return soon.

Figure 2
SAMPLE GUIDELINES FOR TEACHING

1. Develop a simple, natural, conversational style that is comfortable.
   a. You are talking with people, other human beings.
   b. Talk as if you were speaking with one other person.
   c. Look at the audience, individually and collectively.
   d. Interact with the audience and engage their attention.
   e. Make eye contact often as you are speaking and listening.

2. Project your voice so it can be heard by the entire audience.
   a. Let your voice out naturally.
   b. Begin slowly and gradually increase the pitch and volume.
   c. Articulate and enunciate your words clearly.

3. Practice poise, posture, and gesture.
   a. Stand or sit in a comfortable position.
   b. Use the podium, desk, or table if it makes you more at ease.
   c. Relax and move around, but try not to pace.
   d. Use gestures naturally, but try not to overuse them.
   e. Try to be at the audience level or above so you can see the individuals.

4. Be engaged in your teaching.
   a. Show enthusiasm, but be courteous and tasteful at the same time.
   b. Show respect for your audience, but assume nothing from them.
   c. Speak with confidence and authority; you are the expert.
   d. Be prepared and know your subject well; if you don't, admit it.
   e. Organize your material well, but allow for questions.
   f. Make your transitions clear as you move into a new topic.
   g. Summarize your main points at the end of your presentation.

5. Welcome discussion as you proceed, after each point or at the end.
   a. Encourage discussion by being open and approachable.
   b. Repeat the comment or question for clarification.
   c. Encourage the audience to add to your contributions to the discussion.
   d. Be flexible if the audience wants to continue the discussion.

6. Listen carefully to your audience.
   a. Concentrate on what is being said or asked; rephrase if necessary.
   b. Avoid interrupting; everyone needs to be heard.
   c. Listen for what may not be said or asked.
   d. Be patient and understanding.

7. Select aids or audiovisual material only if it is appropriate.
   a. If the aid does not add to the presentation, don't use it.
   b. Practice using the aid and make sure it works effectively.

Figure 2 adapted with permission from Joan Ormondroyd.

SUGGESTED ASSIGNMENTS

ı self-guided tour of a library with script and map from
t-of-view of uninitiated users who have never been in the
; before; or, write a slide/tape script describing either a
; physical arrangement and its services to users, or a
section or department within a library, its physical
arrangement and services.

2. Teach another person how to do something in five minutes. (Cut
an onion, knit a particular stitch, load film in a camera, make a
book cover.) If possible, have yourself videotaped while you are
performing this teaching task. If that is not possible, ask someone
to observe you; or, explain how something works in five minutes
to a group of people (the class if possible). If available, have
yourself videotaped. Ask for critiques in terms of your personal
teaching style: voice level, gestures, body language. Did your
presentation intrude into the content of your mesage? Ask for
evaluations in terms of your subject content: clarity of
explanation, amount of information given. Were you wordy and
complex, or silent and withdrawn?

SUGGESTED READINGS

Dewey, John. *Democracy and Education.* New York: Free Press, 1916.

Frick, Elizabeth. "Information Structure and Bibliographic Instruction." *The Journal of Academic Librarianship* 1 (September 1975): 12-14.

Gagne, Robert Mills. *The Conditions of Learning.* New York: Holt, Rinehart, 1965.

Gattegno, Caleb. *What We Owe Our Children: The Subordination of Teaching to Learning.* New York: Outerbridge and Olenstfrey, 1970.

Hughes, J. Marshal. "Tour of the Library by Audio-Tape." *Special Libraries* 65 (July 1974): 288-90.

Jersild, Arthur T. *When Teachers Face Themselves.* New York: Columbia College, 1955.

Kenney, Donald J. "Role of Technical Services Librarians in Library Instruction." *Southeastern Librarian* 31 (Spring 1981): 11-13.

Kobelski, Pamela, and Mary Reichel. "Conceptual Frameworks for Bibliographic Instruction." *The Journal of Academic Librarianship* 7 (May 1981): 73-77.

Lynch, Beverly P., and Karen S. Siebert. "The Involvement of the Librarian in the Total Educational Process." *Library Trends* 29 (Summer 1980): 127-38.

Lynch, Mary Jo. "Library Tours: The First Step." In *Educating the Library User*, by John Lubans, pp. 254-68. New York: Bowker, 1974.

MacGregor, John, and Raymond G. McInnis. "Integrating Classroom Instruction and Library Research: The Cognitive Functions of Bibliographic Network Structures." *Journal of Higher Education* 98 (January-February 1977): 17-38.

Maxwell, Martha. *Improving Student Learning Skills.* San Francisco, CA: Jossey-Bass, 1979.

Palmer, Millicent. "Creating Slide-Tape Library Instruction; The Librarian's Role." *Drexel Library Quarterly* 8 (July 1972): 251-67.

Pollet, Dorothy, and Peter C. Haskell. *Sign Systems for Libraries: Solving the Wayfinding Problem.* New York: Bowker, 1979.

Postman, Neil. *Teaching as a Conserving Activity.* New York: Delacorte Press, 1980.

Postman, Neil. *Teaching as a Subversive Activity.* New York: Delacorte Press, 1969.

Rader, Hannelore B. "Reference Services as a Teaching Function." *Library Trends* 29 (Summer 1980): 95-103.

Roberts, Anne. "The Changing Role of the Academic Instruction Librarian." *Catholic Library World* 51 (February 1980): 283-85.

Roberts, Anne. "How to Generate User Interest in Library Orientation and Instruction." *Bookmark* 38 (Fall 1979): 228-30.

Roberts, Anne. "Prescriptive, Descriptive, or Proscriptive? Implications of the Developmental Guidelines, a Commitment to Information Services." *RQ* 17 (Spring 1978): 223-25.

Roberts, Anne. "Teaching Librarians to Teach." *Lifeline* 17 (September 1981): 6-7.

Rogers, Carl R. *Freedom to Learn.* Columbus, OH: Charles D. Merrill, 1969.

Simmons, Beatrice D. "Librarian: Instructional Programmer." *Drexel Library Quarterly* 8 (July 1972): 247-50.

Smalley, Topsy N. "Bibliographic Instruction in Academic Libraries: Questioning Some Assumptions." *Journal of Academic Librarianship* 3 (November 1977): 280-83.

Spencer, Robert C. "The Teaching Library." *Library Journal* 103 (May 15, 1978): 1021-24.

Toy, Beverly. "The Role of the Academic Librarian: A Symposium." *Journal of Academic Librarianship* 4 (July 1978): 128-38.

Whitehead, Alfred North. *The Aims of Education.* New York: Mentor Books, 1964.

III
MAKING IT WORK

MODES OF LIBRARY INSTRUCTION

There are various methods of library instruction, and several modes for carrying out these methods. By method is meant the set form or orderly process, procedure, or arrangement for library instruction, such as formal courses, course-integrated instruction, course-related instruction, tutorials, seminars, and mini-courses. By mode is meant the manner of doing the method, such as the lecture, the group discussion, self-directed or self-paced learning, one-to-one interaction, or using print or media.

One should consider users' and librarians' needs when designing an instruction program, and there are several factors which should be considered before selecting either methods or modes for library instruction: the users' needs in terms of when they want the instruction and whether or not they want immediate responses; the librarians' needs in terms of their personalities, and how they fit with the individual methods or modes; the depth of library instruction required by users for their needs; the length of preparation time both for users and for librarians; the amount of time available for participation in the library instruction both by users and by librarians; the effectiveness in terms of user retention; the ease of preparing, revising, or updating materials; the costs; the amount of library staff in terms of time and numbers and the adaptability to evaluation techniques, goals, and objectives. These factors are discussed in Chapter VI of this text.

LECTURE

The modes of teaching can be examined for their applicability in library instruction. The lecture, the most traditional way of presenting information, is a good vehicle for conveying knowledge to users. For the lecture to be effective, it should be well-organized, including an introduction with stated objectives, or an outline of the main body with major points stressed and reviewed, and a conclusion with a summary of the points made. Practice on the topic of the lecture should follow the lecture as closely as possible for reinforcement. As an example, if a lecture describes a search strategy for finding sources in early American history, a follow-up session in using the tools mentioned would strengthen the information just received from the lecture, particularly if it were done immediately following the lecture, or the next day.

There are many advantages to the lecture: a lecture can be prepared and used over and over again with little revision; it is a good way to present information and teach facts; it can be course-related, subject-related, or procedure-related; it can chart the library skills that are necessary to complete an assignment or a particular exercise; it can introduce users to the general library services and the major services or references or resources librarians think users will need; it can be incorporated into several other formats such as walking tours, workshops, or used with print or media presentations, or in particular sections of the library; it can occur in the library, in the classroom, or in lecture halls; and it is a mode that is familiar to most people.

But there are some disadvantages to the lecture: a lecture often tries to do too much at once, creating awareness about library resources, demonstrating the use of these resources, promoting the use of the resources, and establishing rapport with users; it may not always keep the attention of users; it cannot allow for the levels of ability in the users who are all receiving the same information; it is a one-way communication process; it must be timed appropriately and should occur at the point when users are slightly frustrated and have immediate use for the information covered in the lecture; it may not allow for profitable interaction if the group is large; and it may not elicit the enthusiasm and positive response from users that other modes do.

Nevertheless, the lecture continues to be one of the ways instruction librarians teach library skills. The lecture can be used most effectively if certain points are noted. The pace of a lecture should be varied; every ten of fifteen minutes some interruption should occur to maintain user interest, whether it be questions, change of topic, or change of voice. The framework of a lecture should be tied to no more than seven points. The information presented in a lecture should relate directly to the practical application of the lecture topic in a follow-up session.

GROUP DISCUSSION

The group discussion can be effective in library instruction since it involves users as participants in the activity. Group discussion fosters active learning; therefore, the learning that occurs with this mode is quite likely to be retained since some effort was used in acquiring it. For the discussion to be effective, the group size should be from six to eight people, enough to guarantee a variety of skills among the group members. The members should, if possible, choose the other members themselves rather than have them assigned.

There are many advantages to the group discussion mode: it is flexible and can be used in any situation; it lends itself to the idea of the instruction librarian as facilitator; it promotes the retention of learning because of active participation; it makes use of the socialization processes within any group; it is appropriate for practical experiences since users accept responsibility for their own learning of library skills; it is suitable for applying skills to new situations; it is a good mode for problem solving and increasing understanding; and it facilitates an open and communicative atmosphere.

The disadvantages of group discussion are the following: it won't work if the users are incompatible; it has to be carefully organized in order to be effective; it takes involvement by the instruction librarian to be effective; and some users may present resistance to this mode if it is not familiar to them.

Group discussion is becoming increasingly popular with instruction librarians. Since it fosters active participation by learners, it is appropriate for library instruction skills where theory and practice mingle.

SELF-DIRECTED

Self-directed or self-paced learning, also known as individualized instruction, is the type which users may practice independently of the librarians or teachers. Self-directed learning has been developed and used with many adults who were reluctant to participate in instruction with groups but wanted to learn new skills. This mode allows for the structuring of sequences which build on one another naturally, as the learners progress through the instruction. Self-directed learning usually helps users relate the new knowledge and skills they are learning to past experiences and situations. Learning contracts are often used with this mode since they can be designed for the particular situation and needs of the learner. The components for self-directed learning are familiar ones: diagnose learning needs; specify learning objectives; detail learning resources and strategies; state the evidence of accomplishment; and evaluate the learning experience.

There are many advantages to the self-directed mode in library instruction: it can be used at the users' pace and convenience; it can provide immediate reinforcement; it can reach a wide audience; it can teach both the concepts and applications of library skills, such as the search strategy and use of particular reference books; unique sets of exercises or problems can be devised since this mode is geared to the individual; the self-directed mode provides for contact with the librarian at certain intervals; it allows for built-in evaluation; and there are several self-directed or self-paced library skills instructional modules such as slide/tapes or workbooks available commercially.

The disadvantages of the self-directed mode are as follows: users must be motivated to use it; sometimes it tends to focus on small bits of detailed information rather than broad concepts; the material must be updated frequently or revised for individuals; this mode can use a great deal of staff time; the commercial products are expensive and not always appropriate; and the self-directed learning mode in library skills is not always transferable to other library topics or processes.

Self-directed learning has received a great deal of attention in library instruction, particularly through its use in workbooks and computer-assisted instruction. It is certainly one of the more popular modes.

ONE-TO-ONE

The one-to-one mode for library instruction is familiar to most users and librarians. The reference interview and reference service itself have traditionally relied on this mode to the exclusion of all others. The advantages of using it are: individual attention and help are given when needed; there is usually less anxiety for the user; the user becomes familiar with the librarian and comes back frequently for help; and one-to-one interaction for library instruction is comfortable for both user and librarian.

The disadvantages of the one-to-one mode are: it is extremely time-consuming; it requires high-quality staff; it doesn't encourage reluctant users to ask for help; and it may not be effective for teaching the broad concepts of library instruction.

Most librarians and users like this mode for library instruction; the difficulty comes in having appropriate librarians for a high level of service, and in trying to reach large numbers of users.

PRINTED MATERIALS

The use of printed materials for library instruction is very popular. Printed materials, which can be prepared and distributed widely at relatively low cost, range from library orientation tours and explanations of processes to giving directions for using particular tools or for using bibliographies on specific subjects. Most libraries make wide use of printed materials for library instruction purposes.

The advantages of using printed materials are: they can be used in particular situations; they can cover a wide scope of library services and materials; they can explain the use of detailed tools in reference sections as well as search strategies in certain subject disciplines; they are easily updated and can be readily displayed; they are excellent public relations tools for libraries; and some are available commercially.

The disadvantages of using printed materials as a mode for library instruction are as follows: they may require frequent revisions; they are hard to use to teach concepts, selection, or evaluation of materials; they are not flexible; they don't require contact with librarians; they might not be used; the commercial ones may be unsuitable or expensive; and they are time-consuming to prepare initially.

Nevertheless, printed materials can be useful for library instruction. Few libraries produce professional looking materials, although this situation is changing as libraries recognize the importance of marketing their products and services with high-quality, tasteful publications. Publications can give individual libraries an identity by the use of neat, crisp lettering, nice paper, and clean type. Printed materials for libraries have traditionally been in the following categories—tours, self-guided tours, bibliographies, handbooks, maps, workbooks, exercises, and letters—although signs and posters are also used for library instruction.

Librarians should reflect on publications and produce them to fit the needs of their users. It is helpful to ask a few questions when planning printed materials: how will the materials be used (alone, as a supplement)? how will the materials be designed (clarity of text, charts, maps, or diagrams, layout, paper, format)? how will the materials be produced (inhouse, commercially, by style and size of type, color of paper, ink)? and how will the message be conveyed? Instruction librarians can use printed materials profitably if they keep users and their needs in mind when designing publications. Printed materials can be assets in library instruction activities if they are well designed. Figure 3 (see p. 46) illustrates printed guides for library instruction.

AUDIOVISUAL PRESENTATIONS

The use of slide/tapes, audiotapes, and videotapes as audiovisual presentations in library instruction was very popular in the 1970s. Most libraries used these presentations for library orientation or point-of-use.

Audiovisual presentations can reach a large number of users; they can save the constant preparation needed with other modes; multiple copies of audiovisual presentations can be produced for showing in several places; they are appropriate for both large groups and individuals; audiovisual presentations can be excellent public relations tools; and they can combine orientation and instruction.

Audiovisual presentations, however, must be of high quality or no one will watch them; they require technical skills; they are expensive to produce and to maintain; they require expensive equipment; audiovisual productions require outlets and space for presentation; and they may require frequent revision and are very time-consuming to prepare initially.

Audiovisual presentations can be advantageous if appropriate measures are taken first. Guidelines to keep in mind are: which media options will be used (slides, audiotapes, slide/tapes, videotapes); what space and equipment will be required (screens, earphones, caramates, projectors, cassette recorders); what it will cost and who will pay (library, other institution, special fund); how the media presentations will be operated, maintained, and stored; who will revise them; who will write the scripts (keeping them interesting, short, and clear); who will record or take pictures; and who will put the presentation together. Media can be most effective and should be considered for library instruction. Figures 4 and 5 (see pp. 54 and 57) are examples of scripts written to accompany audiovisual presentations on search strategy and government publications.

COMPUTER-ASSISTED INSTRUCTION

Technology, and particularly the computer, presents new challenges to instruction librarians. Most libraries have some form of computerized technology in their operations; it may be acquisition and circulation processes, searching of online data bases, or using computer-assisted instruction as tutorials in teaching users how to implement a system. Whatever the technology employed in libraries, philosophical differences related to the role of the librarian arise. Librarians are seen as either intermediaries or educators in the area of computers. It is the old argument of information vs. instruction.

Computer-assisted instruction (CAI), or computer-aided learning (CAL), is a mode that was particularly popular in the 1970s when money was available for programs and experimentation. The two institutions that fostered CAI and CAL were the University of Illinois and the University of Denver, and much has been written about their programs in the literature. In using these self-instructional modes, three levels for users are apparent: tutorials to begin searching in a step-by-step fashion; assistance during the search if users make errors; and explanation for using the existing systems. Many data bases are developing their own CAI or CAL systems as part of their function rather than relying on printed instruction manuals. The current thrust is for data bases to have their own instructional modules so that users can become their own searchers and the information can be delivered directly to them rather than by the librarian or information specialist. Some data bases which already have their own self-instructional modules built into the online system are:

1. MEDLEARN for MEDLINE

2. CRS for SCORPIO

3. TRAINER for DIALOG and ORBIT

These are only a few examples, and new self-instructional modules are being developed for data bases all the time.

The University of Denver CAI system consists of twenty-one courses as an integral part of reference services. These courses range from how to use indexes and abstracts to how to research a term paper. The Programmed Logic for Automatic Teaching Operation system (PLATO) at the University of Illinois is similar to the Library of Congress system, Subject Content Oriented Retriever for Processing Information Online (SCORPIO). At Illinois, library instruction using computerized self-teaching methods focuses on reference sources and bibliographic access to collections. The PLATO system developed five sections: which reference tool to use in particular situations; how the bibliography of a field is related to its discipline and how that information is disseminated; what the various responsibilities of the library staff are; what kinds of library services are provided by the library; and how to locate particular periodical titles.

There are many advantages to using computer-assisted instruction: learning can be more interesting than with a programmed printed text because of the medium; users can proceed at their own pace and enter programs at their own level of need; users can learn the same amount of information in less time than with some of the more traditional lecture or discussion methods of instruction; users can learn the particular system and how it works while being given instruction in using it; librarians can be freed to do other things; the programs are easy to revise and update; most systems can also provide record-keeping capabilities; the systems can impose sound instructional design on the various learning situations; after the initial costs, most computer-assisted instruction systems are economical to operate; and they can be used in a variety of geographical locations.

There are some disadvantages to using computer-assisted instruction: the beginning costs are expensive; machinery is needed (terminals and computers); and not all data bases have built their own instructional modules into their systems, so that printed manuals are still necessary.

Computer-assisted instruction is cost-effective after the initial equipment costs, since online searching is less expensive than manual searching in terms of professional time and efficiency. It is a mode which will be used even more in the future for library instruction activities as computers become more common.

Figure 3
SAMPLE GUIDES

IF YOU FEEL LIKE SHOOTING YOURSELF, DON'T.
COME TO THE LIBRARY FOR HELP INSTEAD.

We have guides, aids, bibliographies,
and librarians to help you with your
library research problems.

Figure 3 (cont'd)

HOW TO DO RESEARCH IN THE LIBRARY:
A STEP-BY-STEP APPROACH

Step 1.   Look in a general or subject encyclopedia for your topic.

Example: ABORTION

Encyclopedia Americana
International Encyclopedia of the Social Sciences

Step 2.   Break up your topic into smaller subjects.

Example: Psychological effects of abortion
Legal problems with abortion
Social and cultural aspects of abortion
Moral questions about abortion

Step 3.   For any known books on your topic, check in the author/title catalog.

Example: Granfield, David. *The Abortion Decision*, 1969.

Step 4.   Look in the subject catalog for books on your topic.

Example: Abortion
Birth Control

You may have to broaden or narrow your topic to find the appropriate headings. If you have difficulty with the subject headings, check the proper headings used in the *Library of Congress Subject Headings.*

Step 5.   Make sure that you copy down the entire call number on the left-hand corner of the catalog card for each book you want. The call number designates the book's location on the shelf.

Example: RG
136
B349

Step 6.   There are many periodical indexes and abstracts in the reference area designed to help you locate information. The subject ABORTION can be looked up in several indexes.

Example: *Readers' Guide to Periodical Literature*
Social Sciences and Humanities Index
Index to Legal Periodicals
Psychological Abstracts

(Figure 3 continues on page 48.)

Figure 3 (cont'd)

Step 7.   Consult the *Periodicals Collection Dictionary Catalog* to determine which titles the library owns. The "periodical printout" also gives the call numbers for the magazines.

Examples: PER RC 321 P93   *Psychiatry*

PER BF 1 A5   *American Journal of Psychology*

PER RA 421 A42x   *American Journal of Public Health*

PER DS 101 C63   *Commentary*

Please ask a reference librarian if you need help with any step of this process.

HOW TO READ A CALL NUMBER

The call number for a book is that which indicates the specific location of a book in a library. It is made up of letters and numbers in a combination designated by the Library of Congress classification scheme which the University Library uses for organizing and shelving books.

The first letter of a call number refers to the broad class to which the book is assigned. It also provides a location key. Books with call numbers beginning with A-K are shelved on the third floor, and books with call numbers beginning with L-Z are shelved on the second floor.

All libraries have collections which are shelved differently from the main collection. Books with the prefix EXT are in our Downtown Campus Branch Collection, and books with the prefix LIB are in the School of Library and Information Science Collection.

Books within the main library with the prefix REF are in the reference collection; books with the prefix SPE are in special collections; PER indicates that the material is in the periodicals collection. An * indicates that the book is oversized, and a - indicates that the book is undersized; these books are shelved on the second floor in the front wing at the end of the Zs.

There are several nonbook abbreviations that you should know about:

CRD designates microcard;
CDP designates microcard periodical;
FIC indicates microfiche;
FCP indicates microfiche periodical.

These are housed in the microform collection.

There are some prefixes which we no longer use; if you come across them, ignore them, for the books are now shelved in the regular main collection. These obsolete prefixes are: UNI, DCB, HUM, SOC, SCI, BUS, GSP.

Figure 3 (cont'd)

The Library of Congress classification scheme uses a combination of letters and numbers to indicate the specific subject of the book and its author.

Example: A book entitled *The Sanctity of Life and the Criminal Law*, written by Glanville Llewelyn Williams, would be classified

KF   (law is the main subject)
9300   (number used to further describe subject)
W54x (author and book number)

The first line of a call number is always a letter or letters. The second line of a call number is always a number ranging from 1 through 9999. The third line of a call number is a book number or author number. This line should be treated as if it were a decimal, so that W54x would come on the shelf before W6.

Some of the books in the library are shelved in designated areas; the materials shelved in these areas are color coded, and the catalog cards for these materials have colored plastic covers which correspond to colored taped on the spine of the books:

Red indicates that the book is shelved in the law area in the first floor front wing.

Blue indicates that the book is shelved in the ready reference area near the reference desk.

Green indicates that the book is shelved in the government publications area.

Black indicates that the book is shelved in the abstract and index area.

To find this particular book, you would go up to the third floor where the circulating Ks are, since there is no plastic cover on the catalog card, and go until you find the KF section. Then you would begin the second line and find the 9000s and go until you come to KF 9300. You would then proceed with the third line, going from A-W until you come to KF 9300 W54x.

Remember to ask the librarians for help if you are confused or have questions about call numbers.

HOW TO INTERPRET A CATALOG CARD

The University Library uses the Library of Congress classification system, which combines letters and numbers in a way that designates subjects for organizing books. The books in the University Library are shelved according to this LC system. Using the first letter of the call number as a guide, consult the location directory to see what floors the books are on.

(Figure 3 continues on page 50.)

Figure 3 (cont'd)

Library of Congress Classification System:

A	General Works
B-BJ	Philosophy, Psychology
BL-BX	Religion
C	Auxiliary Sciences of History
D	History: General and Old World (Eastern Hemisphere)
E-F	History: American (Western Hemisphere)
G	Geography, Anthropology, Recreation
H	Social Sciences, Statistics, Economics, Sociology
J	Political Science
KD	Law of the United Kingdom and Ireland
KF	Law of the United States
L	Education
M	Music, Books on Music
N	Fine Arts, Architecture
P-Pa	General Philology and Linguistics, Classical Languages and Literature
PA Supplement	Byzantine and Modern Greek Literature, Medieval and Modern Latin Literature
PB-PH	Modern European Languages
PG	Russian Literature
PJ-PM	Languages and Literatures of Asia, Africa, Oceania, American Indian Languages, Artificial Languages
P-PM Supplement	Index to Languages and Dialects
PN, PR, PS, PZ	General Literature, English and American Literature, Fiction in English, Juvenile Literature
PQ, Part 1	French Literature
PQ, Part 2	Italian, Spanish, and Portuguese Literature
PT, Part 1	German Literature
PT, Part 2	Dutch and Scandinavian Literature
Q	Science, Mathematics
R	Medicine
S	Agriculture, Plants, Animal Industry
T	Technology
U	Military Science
V	Naval Science
Z	Bibliography, Library Science

Figure 3 (cont'd)

The card catalog is divided into an author/title section and a subject section. A card catalog has useful information on it.

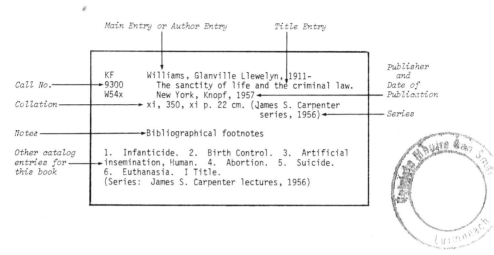

The main entry or author entry is probably the key item to look for on a catalog card. An author may be a person, place, institution, or corporation. This element extends the farthest out to the left on the card. The title entry is an important part of the catalog card. Often a work may be listed only by title. The publisher and the publishing date may be important if authority or currency is desired. The series listing tells whether or not the work is part of a series.

The call number is the number in the left-hand corner of the card which designates the book's location in the library according to the Library of Congress classification system.

The collation gives the size, pagination, and other physical dimensions of the work; it also tells if a book is illustrated with plates or portraits. The notes section can tell you unusual features about a book and whether or not it has a bibliography.

A crucial part of the catalog card is "other catalog entries for this book." The Arabic numerals tell you what subject headings are used for this work, and the Roman numerals tell you what author or title headings are used for the book. If you wanted books on a similar topic, you could check the subject catalog under the designated subject headings.

If you have any questions about this process, ask at the reference desk.

(Figure 3 continues on page 52.)

Figure 3 (cont'd)

HOW TO LOCATE PERIODICAL ARTICLES

The University Library reference area has many periodical indexes which group articles by subject. Use an index to look up the subject of the topic you are researching. One index that is very useful is the *Social Sciences Index*.

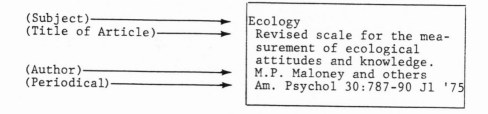

The subject is ecology. The name of the *article* is "Revised scale for the measurement of ecological attitudes and knowledge." The author is M. P. Maloney and others. The name of the periodical is *American Psychologist*. Only the abbreviation is given in the citation.

A complete list of abbreviations is given at the front of each index. Be sure to check these and get the full title of the periodical you want *before* you check to see if the library owns it. Abbreviations can be confusing, as many titles seem alike. The volume of the periodical you want is 30, and the article itself is on pages 787-90 of the July 1975 issue.

Now that you have written down all this information, you must determine whether or not the library owns the periodical. Consult the *Periodicals Collection Dictionary Catalog*, commonly called the "periodical printout." Copies of these are at the reference desk in the Periodicals Room. Note the instructions on the front of the catalog; they tell you how the titles are alphabetized. Locate the title of the periodical *American Psychologist* in the printout. This is how the entry looks:

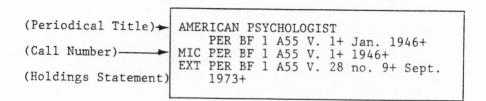

The basic call number for this title is BF 1 A55. It is listed three times with three different prefixes to indicate various locations and forms of this title. "PER" by itself means the title is a periodical in hard copy and located on the shelves in the Periodicals Room. "MIC" means the title is on microfilm and

Figure 3 (cont'd)

housed in the microforms area. "EXT" designates a hard copy of a title at the branch or extension library. (There are other prefixes for other forms and locations.)

Copy the call number and look at the holdings statement to see if the library has the date you need. The holdings statement, V. 1 + 1946 +, tells you that the library starts with volume 1 published in 1946 and has everything to date, that is the latest issues. You will notice that EXT has nothing before September 1973. The seven digit numbers at the right of the entry are for library use only; just ignore them.

Once you have gotten the call number, go to the stacks in the Periodicals Room or to the microforms area to find the issue you need. In the stacks, both bound and loose issues are shelved together according to the Library of Congress call numbers. Using the first letter of the call number as a guide, locate the "B" section of the Periodicals Room. Continue on until you come to "BF." The next line is "1." After you find "BF 1" you must next locate "A55." The last line is shelved as if it contained a decimal before the last digit, A5.5; therefore, A55 shelves before A6. Microfilm reels are kept in cabinets, but you follow the same procedure, using the call number, to locate the one you want.

Once you understand the basics of how to use an index and how to physically locate periodicals on the shelf, you should have no trouble locating the materials you need. If you are unable to locate what you need, please consult the staff at the periodicals information desk.

If you have any questions about the process, ask at either the reference desk or the information desk.

Figure 4
THE SEARCH STRATEGY SCRIPT

Let's face it. The library can be a pretty confusing place. It contains more information than you, the student, could possibly want; but unless you have a search strategy for uncovering needed materials, you can feel defeated before you even start looking. Say, what is this search strategy, anyway? A search strategy is like a roadmap—it shows you the correct road to take, suggests what to look for along the way, and assures you that you will arrive at your destination. Following a search strategy to locate library literature for a research paper can help you in at least three different ways: First, it can help you choose the scope of your topic. Without determining the exact breadth of your topic before beginning your research, you could end up with a monumental topic that would be appropriate for a thousand page paper; or, such a narrow topic that you can locate little previous research on the subject. Second, a search strategy can help you avoid aimless searching, by focusing your attention on the appropriate sources to use. Third, it ensures that you don't miss something important, by directing you step by step through the different methods of discovering appropriate books and magazine articles on your topic.

The first step in an organized search strategy is to determine your topic and define the exact scope you plan to cover in your paper. A good place to look for an overview of a topic which interests you is in a general, or a subject, encyclopedia where articles can give you a good idea of how the topic is organized and what particular aspects might be appropriate for a research paper. This article, for instance, could help you narrow your topic from the broad area of "pacifism" to the more easily handled narrower topic of "pacifism in the 1960's and 1970's." After determining the scope of your paper, you can also use the introductory articles in the encyclopedia to help you draft a tentative outline organizing your topic. Check the bibliographies at the end of the articles too. Although some professors question the use of encyclopedias as source materials, they can be very helpful in identifying some of the classic texts that stand as the authoritative works on your topic. An introduction, an organization of content, an overview of the topic, and some preliminary sources—all this from one encyclopedia article.

Now you are ready to begin your research for appropriate books. Use the author-title catalog to locate any known sources. You will use the subject catalog to locate the rest of your books. Begin your subject search by consulting the *Library of Congress Subject Headings* list, which will tell you the correct forms of subjects used in our catalog. You first locate the entry for the word "pacifism." Noting that the word is in bold print, you are assured that the word is, indeed, a correct Library of Congress subject heading. The scope note describes the term and gives you the clue to check other subjects as well, such as the word "peace" for information on peace movements. Additional subjects are suggested by the "see also" section. The terms indicated by an "xx" either duplicate what you find under the "see also" section, or are more general than your original term. They may, or may not, be of help to you. Let's take one of the more appropriate "see also" references and check in the subject book for its entry. Again, you find the term in bold

Figure 4 reprinted by permission of Melodye Morrison Khattak.

Figure 4 (cont'd)

type, indicating that it is a correct term which can be used as a subject in the catalog. Notice also the additional information that the term "conscientious objectors" can be used as a subdivision under names of wars. That particular bit of information leads us to this entry, dealing with conscientious objectors during the Vietnam War. As you are using the subject book, be sure to jot down all of these possible terms to check in the subject catalog. They will be invaluable for locating books on your topic.

Now you are ready to begin your search of the subject catalog. When you locate an interesting book, check the publication date to make sure it is current enough for your topic. If the book seems appropriate, copy down its complete call number so you will be able to locate the book on the shelf. Although you need only the call number to locate the book on the shelf, it is always a good idea to note briefly the author and title as well, in case you need that information later. Also, take a look at the tracings of each card. These tell you what subjects have been used in the catalog to describe these books. You may be able to add to your list of appropriate subject headings by checking the tracings of cards you encounter. After searching in the subject catalog under all pertinent subject headings, you undoubtedly have accumulated a large number of call numbers for books on your topic. Now, with your list of call numbers in hand, you are ready to tackle the stacks. Locate the corresponding books on the shelves. Be sure to check other books shelved near the book you have located. Books sharing a common classification number are likely to be on the same subject, and one of these neighboring books may be even more pertinent than the book you first located. Examine each book carefully for its relevance. Titles can be misleading. Keep track of any books you cannot find on the shelves. By presenting an author and title to the circulation desk attendant, you can discover if a book has already been checked out. You can ask to have it saved for you upon its return, or request that a search be made for the book if there is no record of its being out in circulation. You can see why it was wise to copy down the author and title for each book while you were at the subject catalog—you don't have to search through the catalog again. The bibliographies included in some of the books you have found in the stacks are likely to give you more leads to additional sources of information on your topic. Any important book not owned by the library can be requested from another library by initiating an interlibrary loan.

Once you have selected a number of circulating books to use in your research, you may wish to consult with a reference librarian concerning any relevant books in the reference collection. The librarian can direct you to handbooks, specialized dictionaries and encyclopedias, and bibliographies pertinent to your topic. At this point you can be fairly confident that you have adequately searched the book collection. But what about that vast, unexplored territory called the periodical collection? There are two methods for locating appropriate periodical articles. There is the good old "thumb and hope" method. Thumbing through all the magazines on the shelves may be a very good way of strengthening your thumbs, but it is hardly the most direct way of locating appropriate periodical articles. Let's go back upstairs to the reference collection, where there are some important items you will want to know about. There are numerous periodical indexes in the reference collection, each designed to help you locate magazine articles in a particular subject area. One of the most helpful indexes is the *Social Sciences and Humanities Index.* As its

(Figure 4 continues on page 56.)

Figure 4 (cont'd)

title suggests, this index covers the social sciences and humanities fields. In 1974 it was divided into two sections: the *Social Sciences Index* and the *Humanities Index*. Let's take a look at the *Social Sciences Index*. But don't expect to find the same subject headings used in the periodical indexes as were used in the card catalog. Each index will use its own set of vocabulary, which may or may not be similar to the terminology used in the subject catalog. Here we do find "pacifism," which was a Library of Congress subject heading; but this one, "passive resistance," is a new term to us. Notice that under each subject there is a list of relevant articles, each citation containing full bibliographical information to help you locate it. Periodical titles are often abbreviated in the citations, but a complete list of periodicals indexed can be found at the front of every index. By checking here you can discover the correct name for each periodical abbreviation you encounter.

In order to guarantee that you find the articles you want, be sure to copy down complete bibliographical information for each citation, including the full name of the periodical, volume, number, date, and page. Abbreviations can be confusing, as many titles sound alike. Consulting with the librarian is a good way of discovering pertinent periodical indexes to use for your topic. The librarian might suggest the *New York Times Index*, especially if you are interested in reading a newspaper account of a certain event the way it was described at the time of its happening. This index, listing articles appearing in the *New York Times* newspaper, also has a subject approach. You can see that the subjects tend to be quite complex. Articles within a subject are listed in chronological order. A typical entry summarizes the content of the article, then lists the date, page, and column of the paper where the article may be found. The year is never listed in the citation, as each volume of the index contains citations for only one year. Another appropriate index for this topic would be the *Public Affairs Information Services Bulletin*, commonly known as *PAIS*. This index covers the areas of government, economics, political science, and international affairs, and includes not only periodical articles, but pamphlets, books, and government documents, such as this Senate hearing. In order to locate this document, it is necessary to go to the government publications section of the library. A librarian can help you to locate the specific document you need. Now that you have a complete list of possible periodical articles to consult, you are ready to tackle that periodical collection.

First item on the agenda is to copy down the call number for each periodical you wish to locate. *Periodical Collection Lists* such as this one are prominently displayed on tables in the periodical room. They give call numbers for every periodical found here. After determining the call numbers you need, you are ready to enter the periodical stacks. Since you have copied down a complete citation for each item, you should have no trouble locating the articles you need.

This search strategy has provided you with an organized path to follow so that the research for, and the writing of, a research paper can be a structured procedure rather than a haphazard affair. And the library can be a storehouse of information, to which you now hold the key.

Figure 5
THE GOVERNMENT PUBLICATIONS SCRIPT

The government publications section of the University Library contains federal, state, international, and foreign documents. Most of the material in the area is not listed in the card catalog of the library. Various indexes which are used to locate materials are in the government publications section. It is necessary to use these indexes to locate materials in this area. If you are looking for a specific publication of a government agency, or if you are trying to find information which a governmental office might have published on a particular subject, ask at the government publications desk. The University Library has been a selective depository for United States documents since 1965. This means that only publications in certain selected subject areas are received.

Access to United States documents is provided by the *Monthly Catalog of United States Government Publications.* This is a monthly listing of U.S. documents available through the Government Printing Office, arranged by issuing agency with a subject index. There is a cumulative annual index as part of the December issue. The hard copy documents that the library owns are shelved by the Superintendent of Documents Classification Number, which is usually called the "Sudoc" number. The library also has all of the publications which are listed in the *Monthly Catalog* since 1962 in microprint. Not all U.S. government publications are listed in the *Monthly Catalog*, and therefore some documents may not be available in the University Library. There are other indexes which describe and retrieve these documents and they will be discussed later on. Once you have located a citation in the *Monthly Catalog*, the librarian will help you to find the material. The government publications section maintains a record of all hard copy publications which it receives. The librarian can check this record to see if the library has the publication, and where it is located. If the material you want is not available in hard copy and was published after 1962, you may use it in microprint. The librarian will show you how to locate the microprint and how to use the appropriate reader.

There are several other tools to help you use U.S. government publications. *The Cumulative Subject Index to the Monthly Catalog of U.S. Government Publications* is located next to the *Monthly Catalog* and is, as its name suggests, a subject index to the *Monthly Catalog* for the period 1900-1971. There are also decennial, or ten-year, personal author indexes to the *Monthly catalog* for the period 1941-1970. *The United States Government Manual*, an annual publication, lists the government's organizations and describes their functions. *CIS Index*, published by Congressional Information Service, is a monthly listing of congressional publications with abstracts and indexes. *American Statistics Index (ASI)* provides subject and category indexes to statistical information published by the U.S. government. For assistance in using these indexes, ask at the government publications desk. The library has some National Technical Information Service publications. NTIS is the "central source for the publication and sale of government sponsored research and development reports." *Government Reports Announcement and Index* provides selected abstracts of NTIS research reports. Since 1974 the library has subscribed to *Selected Reports in Microfiche*, a service which

(Figure 5 continues on page 58.)

Figure 5 reprinted by permission of Carolyn Jean Colwell.

Figure 5 (cont'd)

provides microfiche copies of NTIS documents in selected subject areas. The areas which the library receives microfiche for are: atmospheric sciences, management practice, management research, transportation, behavior and society, library and information science, and business and economics. The government publications section contains the documents of the Educational Resources Information Center (ERIC). These materials, referred to as ERIC, are research reports in education broadly defined. For example: language, linguistics, educational administration and library science are included. *Resources in Education* provides abstracts for ERIC documents, and indexes them by subject, author, and institution. There are cumulative annual indexes, as well as indexes that cover the years 1966-1969, and 1970-1971. Most documents listed in ERIC are available in microfiche in the library. The microfiche is arranged by ED or "educational document" number, as listed in *Resources in Education*. The librarian will help you to locate and use these documents.

The University Library collects state and municipal documents. Although the collection is not large, the library is attempting to acquire all New York state publications in areas that support the university's curriculum. Documents from other states and from major U.S. cities are acquired selectively. Access to this collection is provided by a card catalog located in the government publications area. Like publications of the U.S. government, these publications are shelved by a classification number which is derived from the agency's name. The government publications section has United Nations publications. There are a limited number of publications in hard copy. In addition, most U.N. documents are available in microprint. The *United Nations Documents Index* provides access to this collection. The University Library has been a depository for the publications of the Commission of the European Communities since 1973. The library also receives publications of many other international agencies and foreign countries. Most of the international and foreign documents in the library are part of the library's general collections and are listed in the card catalog; but some of these documents are located in the government publications area — for example the British House of Commons papers.

Many hard copy publications in the government publications area circulate, and may be charged out at the circulation desk. Although the microform publications must be used in the library, there are machines in the periodical room which will make hard copy from fiche. Government publications unavailable in the library may be requested by initiating an interlibrary loan request. As you can see, there are many kinds of documents which provide a wide variety of information. Access to these materials is complex, and may be confusing. For any assistance in locating and using government publications in the library, ask the librarian at the government publications desk.

SUGGESTED ASSIGNMENTS

1. Outline a library lecture on either general library processes or on subject resources and tools for a particular group. Keep in mind the points covered in the text for preparing good lectures: no more than seven points covered; vary the pace, etc.

2. Design a "how to" handout for a specific action for users in a library; you may use charts, diagrams, or illustrations. Remember to keep it simple, clear, and understandable.

SUGGESTED READINGS

Adams, Mignon. "Individualized Approach to Learning Library Skills." *Library Trends* 29 (Summer 1980): 83-94.

Benson, Stanley. "Has Education Ever Gotten ... So Little for So Much?" *Learning Today* 12 (Winter 1981): 40-46.

Brown, James W. *AV Instruction: Technology, Media, and Methods.* New York: McGraw-Hill, 1977.

Culkin, Patricia B. "Computer-Based Public Access Systems: A Forum for Library Instruction." *Drexel Library Quarterly* 16 (January 1980): 69-82.

Culkin, Patricia B. "Instructional Materials: Design and Development. Computer-Assisted Instruction in Library Use." *Drexel Library Quarterly* 8 (July 1972): 301-311.

Dudley, Miriam. *Workbook in Library Skills: A Self-Directed Course in the Use of UCLA's College Library.* Los Angeles: University of California, College Library, 1973.

Hardesty, Larry, and Frances Gatz. "Application of Instructional Development to Mediated Library Instruction." *Drexel Library Quarterly* 16 (January 1980): 3-26.

Hardesty, Larry. *Use of Slide/Tape Presentations in Academic Libraries.* New York: Jeffrey Norton, 1978.

Katz, William. *Your Library: A Reference Guide.* New York: Holt, 1979.

Knapp, Sara D. "Instructing Library Patrons about Online Reference Services." *Bookmark* 38 (Fall 1979): 237-42.

Knowles, Malcolm. *The Modern Practice of Adult Education*, rev. ed. Chicago: Follet, 1980.

Knowles, Malcolm. *Self-Directed Learning: A Guide for Learners and Teachers.* New York: Press Association, 1975.

Kupersmith, John. "Informational Graphics and Sign Systems as Library Instruction Media." *Drexel Library Quarterly* 16 (1980): 54-68.

Lawrence, Gail Herndon. "The Computer as an Instructional Device: New Directions for Library User Education." *Library Trends* 29 (Summer 1980): 139-52.

Lolley, John L. "Videotape Programs." *Drexel Library Quarterly* 16 (January 1980): 83-102.

Martin, Jess A.; Joan M. Marcotte; and John E. Baxter. "PLATO in the Library." *Southeastern Librarian* 31 (Spring 1981): 14-15.

Tassia, Margaret, "It's Not Just a Game." *School Library Journal* 25 (March 1979): 105-106.

Tough, Allen. *The Adult's Learning Projects*, 2nd ed. Austin, TX: Learning Concepts, 1979.

Williams, Mitsuko, and Elisabeth B. Davis. "Evaluation of PLATO Library Instructional Lessons." *Journal of Academic Librarianship* 5 (March 1979): 14-19.

IV
TRYING IT OUT

METHODS OF LIBRARY INSTRUCTION

The various modes for doing library instruction have been discussed. The lecture, the group discussion, self-directed or self-paced learning, one-to-one interaction, the use of print or media, and computer-assisted instruction as modes in library instruction can all be used singly or in combinations with each other. It is important to remember that although the material being presented in library instruction is familiar to the librarian, it may not be so for the user. It is important to vary the modes and even the methods to keep the presentations fresh and interesting. In this way, the instruction librarian, as well as the users, is learning and the information is more likely to be demonstrated in a lively fashion.

The most common methods, the set forms or orderly processes, procedures, or arrangements for library instruction, are: formal courses, course-integrated instruction, course-related instruction, tutorials, seminars, mini-courses, point of use and workbooks. Each of these methods will be examined for strengths and weaknesses, advantages and disadvantages, in order to provide an array of forms to consider.

FORMAL COURSES

A familiar method for most people in any kind of instruction is the course. Formal courses in library instruction are fairly common and range from basic courses in bibliography and library research skills to more subject-oriented ones such as those found in education, history, literature, the sciences, government documents, law, and theology. The disadvantages of formal courses are: they may not reach all who need them and therefore the audience is limited; course results may not be readily apparent immediately; they require time, energy, and effort to prepare; they may cause scheduling problems involving librarians, users, and administrators; and they require financial and institutional support. The advantages of formal courses are: they can be designed and prepared initially without continual revising; they may be shaped to fit the users; they may be team taught; they may be designed by some librarians and taught by other librarians; they can be adjusted to meet the users' levels of sophistication; and they provide both immediate and extended interactions between users and librarians.

Librarians can readily see whether or not their users are comprehending the instruction in the formal setting, and a wide variety of formats may be used in courses.

Most formal courses provide some kind of academic credit which dignifies and adds prestige to library instruction. Basic library instruction courses contain similar components (textbooks, readings, audiovisual materials, lectures, guides, worksheets, exercises, quizzes, exams, pre-tests, post-tests, bibliographies, projects), and cover familiar topics (physical orientation to the library building, introduction to library services, library classification schemes, library subject headings, the card catalog, reference materials, periodical indexes, periodical abstracts, newspaper indexes, microforms, government documents, computerized data base searching, interlibrary loan and networking systems, the search strategy process, topic selection, bibliographic citations, footnotes, annotations and compilations, and evaluation of library research sources).

Users and librarians alike find the formal course a good method for library instruction. Users like having a structured sequence of learning experiences with reinforcement by readings and exercises. They also like the practical applications they can make in their library instruction sessions within the course. Librarians find it satisfying to watch their users progress in their research ability in the library while they take the course, and they find the course to be a good way to check on their teaching effectiveness. Librarians like the combination of lecture, discussion, and workshop format that exists in most formal courses. A sample course outline, syllabus, and worksheets that illustrate the nature of most basic library research skills courses are included as Figure 6 (see p. 67). Figure 7 (p. 74) is a sample outline of an advanced course in library research.

COURSE-RELATED, COURSE-INTEGRATED

Course-related library instruction and course-integrated library instruction that provide for user education in libraries are part of the same continuum. Course-related instruction, the usual method of library instruction offered in libraries, provides users with information or teaches them ways to find information to meet the requirements of the course. It often consists of orientation in the form of a tour, a lecture on the most appropriate tools for the course topics, and an exercise to reinforce what has been learned from the tour and the lecture. Course-integrated instruction goes one step further; the library instruction is a necessary part of the course, and the course objectives and course design are built on the library instruction assignments. Often the librarian and teacher work together as a team in conducting the course. Figure 8 (see p. 76) is an example of a form used to request library orientation and instruction sessions.

There are many advantages to course-related library instruction: the library assignments become part of the instruction for the course and can help users understand the course subject's literature, its structure, and effective methods of researching it; the library instruction reinforces the course content, since the library sessions occur with the cooperation and support of the instructor during class time; the library instruction can be flexible and inserted into the course at various times; large numbers of users can be reached easily this way; the library instruction encourages interaction between the users and the librarian after the course is over; and this method helps in building up a library instruction program gradually and successfully.

There are some disadvantages to course-related library instruction: the library instruction may place increased demands on both library staff and library materials; the costs are high in terms of staff and personnel; not all users are reached through this method; many librarians lack training in teaching so this method places burdens on the few who are able and willing, or else certain areas just aren't covered by the library instruction; the library instruction may be difficult to schedule with this method since the peak may come at the same time for all courses; librarians cannot always see the results of their instruction; librarians may become oversaturated in conducting the same library instruction sessions; and often there is too little time to do much actual library instruction using this method.

Nevertheless, this method of course-related instruction can have a large impact on the courses themselves, the students, and even the curriculum, by exposing both students and faculty to sophisticated research skills and to a wider range of library materials than they normally would have used. Course-related instruction can be a great image builder for both the library as the center for learning and knowledge and the librarian as a serious researcher and professional interested in furthering the teaching-learning process. Librarians get to know faculty and students more intimately and can offer suggestions on teaching and researching procedures. This method is one which lends itself well to a wide variety of modes. And course-related instruction can lead into course-integrated library instruction.

Course-integrated library instruction is probably best known at Earlham College in Richmond, Indiana, where library instruction has been taken seriously since 1965. Evan Farber, the library director, has worked closely with faculty and hired his librarians with library instruction uppermost in his mind. The fact that the college is a small, liberal arts, religiously based (Society of Friends) institution also influences the atmosphere. But course-integrated library instruction is not just the domain of the small liberal arts colleges; course-integrated instruction also exists at the University of Georgia, the University of South Carolina, the University of Tennessee, and the University of Washington, to name just a few large academic institutions.

Course-integrated library instruction involves the library from the very beginning with course objectives. Most programs build on sequences which are patterned after the search strategy concept. At Earlham there are four sequences. First, the students take a pre-test in the library. Secondly, each student must do a paper for a required course in humanities which involves basic sources, such as the *Library of Congress Subject Headings, Book Review Digest, Social Sciences and Humanities Index, Public Affairs Information Services, Essay and General Literature Index, Biography Index,* and the *New York Times Index,* and a librarian helps with the bibliography and the paper. The third level involves choosing a literary work, exploring it in relationship to events at the time it was written, in relationship to the critics, and in relationship to the author's life. The fourth level is the seminar paper and is interdisciplinary. There are flexibility and variety in assignments, so that there can be as much or as little structure as desired.

TUTORIALS, SEMINARS, AND MINI-COURSES

Tutorials, seminars, and mini-courses were employed in the 1960s and 1970s, drawing on the interest and enthusiasm of users before many structured library instruction programs had been established. A series of library sessions is given, either on particular topics or processes, or according to individual needs, usually ranging from four to twenty hours. Term paper clinics and workshops on search strategies are examples of how tutorials, seminars, and mini-courses can be used. Often librarians and instructors can work together using these methods, particularly when complemented with study skills, writing skills, and counseling skills. An entire class may attend tutorials, seminars, or mini-courses which have been especially designed for them.

The advantages of this method of library instruction are: it can be based relatively easily on the users' needs; it can be available when the users need the information; it allows for close personal contact; it permits immediate reinforcement and results; it is a method that combines well with workbooks or exercises; and it doesn't require special facilities in terms of space or machinery.

The disadvantages of this method of library instruction are: it can be very time-consuming and difficult to schedule; it may reach a limited audience; it can require expertise that the librarian may not have; it may overwhelm the library in terms of demand (or else no one will appear); and often the series of library sessions using this method overload library resources since very heavy use may be made of both library facilities and materials for short periods of time.

POINT-OF-USE

Point-of-use explanations in library instruction may be either printed materials or audiovisual presentations, usually audiotape or slide/tape, which give information on how to use a particular library tool, such as the card catalog, *Psychological Abstracts*, or the *Readers' Guide to Periodical Literature*. Figure 9 (see p. 77) offers an example of point-of-use to explain the card catalog. Point-of-use instructions can be placed near or next to the tool they are explaining. They are also available when they are needed. Point-of-use explanations can reach many users, and can be repeated as often as the users want.

Many printed point-of-use instructions are commercially available and can simply be laminated and placed next to the tool since they are describing the tool itself and not the particular library. Security may be a problem if the point-of-use materials are audiovisual presentations and require equipment. As in most cases with library instruction modes, point-of-use explanations work most effectively when used in conjunction with other approaches, such as sessions in applying the particular tool to real situations for reinforcement. Point-of-use explanations are versatile and flexible and are used frequently by librarians in library instruction.

WORKBOOKS

Workbooks are popular tools for instruction librarians, particularly in institutions with large populations to reach or with groups of users who have special difficulties. Miriam Dudley of the University of California at Los Angeles

(UCLA) was the first instruction librarian to use the workbook method in library instruction. Her *Workbook in Library Skills*, which she developed for Mexican-Americans, soon became the model for others around the country. Dudley wanted to give these users basic orientation and library instruction. The first step is the physical location of several points: bathrooms, water fountain, pencil sharpener, reference desk, circulation desk, interlibrary loan office, reference collection (especially dictionaries and encyclopedias), periodical indexes, and any other area which would be important to users unfamiliar with libraries. The design of most workbooks is similar; each chapter covers a special topic, beginning with the physical layout and then moving to discrete tools such as the card catalog, periodical indexes, and particular reference tools such as encyclopedias. Some workbooks are basic while others build on the foundation sources and lead the users to more complex skills like the search strategy. What began as a way to assist people with cultural and language differences has continued as a method to help all library users.

Workbooks allow users to feel comfortable with themselves in the library, and to set their own pace. Most workbooks have a running text for directions and explanations with different examples for the exercises. The exercises are meant to be completed serially as assignments, turned in at an appropriate point, reviewed by an instruction librarian, and then returned to the users. There is usually some contact between the librarian and users.

There are other advantages to the workbook approach in teaching library skills and library techniques. Perhaps the most important one is that workbooks make the users active learners, for they are required to perform certain tasks in the library. Workbooks provide an ongoing feedback to the users so they know when and where they are having difficulties with library problems. Workbooks also give users a feeling of accomplishment, since they eventually complete them successfully. The professional appearance of the workbook contrasts to that of most exercises and helps lend a feeling of importance to the task at hand. On a more practical note, workbooks, as they are used currently, are relatively easy to administer.

Workbooks as teaching tools are flexible and can be used in any type of library from large to small, academic to school, or public to special libraries. Workbooks can also be self-supporting, since most library users are willing to buy an instructional aid which can be used as a review book. As a method for library instruction, workbooks use staff time efficiently and can be checked easily and revised periodically. Workbooks used in library instruction programs provide users with immediate reinforcement and they permit learning to occur which is not connected to the personality or teaching style of an individual instruction librarian. They also help take advantage of the sound teaching principle of giving users small amounts of information to learn frequently, rather than large amounts all at once. This permits easy retention of the information on the part of the users, and also makes it easier for the instruction librarians since they can see the progress of their users reflected in the workbooks. Most workbooks call for concrete action, repeated procedures, progressive activities, and specific detailed instructions which teach thought processes. Workbook topics can be used together as individual units, or as sequential progressions of skill mastery, depending upon the situation.

Workbooks provide for built-in conferences between instructors and users since the assignments are checked periodically before their completion. This continual assessment, both for users and instruction librarians, helps to eliminate much of the anxiety in the teaching-learning process, since a record is maintained of the library skills activities in the workbooks.

There are disadvantages in using the workbook approach as a teaching tool. It may not work as a teaching method with all library users. Workbooks may be viewed as impersonal or as busywork, especially if there is no human interaction along the way. The writing and compiling of workbooks can be tiring and burdensome on the library staff. Good staff relations are necessary for the enterprise.

Workbooks for library instruction were initially conceived for users with particular problems. They are far more effective in a structured group setting, like a classroom, with periodic contact between the instructors and the users, than they are when users work on them alone. There is evidence to suggest that the more traditional teaching situation may get better results with the workbook approach than the individualized teaching mode for which it was originally intended. In any event, workbooks are currently one of the key methods used by librarians in different types of libraries to impart library research skills. What began as a technique for teaching basic library orientation skills and remedial work in several areas, has become effective in teaching library research skills in specialized areas such as public policy, history, and anthropology, and in competency-based skills, including computation, writing, and library use.

Instruction librarians have wide experiences in using workbooks, and many community colleges, colleges, and universities have adopted this method as their main approach towards library instruction. Elementary and secondary schools have long used workbooks as an integral part of the curriculum. Teachers and school librarians have worked together designing workbooks and integrating library materials and skills with the subject matter being taught. Workbooks in academic subjects often provide different approaches and ideas for instruction librarians to adapt in workbooks for library instruction skills. Workbooks for teaching library skills have worked well for many instruction librarians in the past, and will probably continue to be used. Examples from a library skills workbook are contained in Figure 10 (see p. 79).

Figure 6
SAMPLE BASIC COURSE

IF YOU DREAD FACING LIBRARY RESEARCH,
REGISTER FOR LIBRARY RESEARCH
LIB 350, Tuesdays, Thursdays
9:45-11:00 a.m. in B14, Library
Taught by reference librarian, Anne Roberts

(Figure 6 continues on page 68.)

Figure 6 (cont'd)

Dear Colleagues:

Our experience shows that many students have difficulty using the University Library in doing their research assignments. As a possible solution to this problem, we have designed a "Library Research" course, LIB 350, for one credit, pass/fail. Our objective is to provide students with a basic understanding of the library so that materials and time may be used efficiently and effectively when doing library research.

Our scope is to help students make efficient use of time and library materials by acquainting them with the physical orientation to the library, the Library of Congress classification scheme, subject headings, reference tools, periodical indexes and abstracts, government documents, information retrieval, search strategy processes and compiling and annotating bibliographies.

We hope this will be a valuable and useful course and ask that you bring it to the attention of your students. Thank you.

Sincerely yours,

Anne Roberts
Associate Librarian
Coordinator of Library
Instruction

Course:	Library Research (LIB 350)

Meeting Times:	Tuesdays, Thursdays 9:45-11:00 a.m.
	Mondays 6:00-9:00 p.m.
	Second Five Weeks of Semester:
	    October 4th-November 3rd
	    October 3rd-October 31st

Room:	University Library, B14
Instructor:	Anne Roberts
Telephone:	457-3347

TEXT: *Manual for the Writers of Term Papers, Theses, Dissertations*, Kate L. Turabian, 4th ed. 1973. Price $2.95. Available in University Bookstore in the non-textbook section.

CREDIT: One unit, pass/fail, no prerequisites.

Figure 6 (cont'd)

COURSE OBJECTIVE:

To provide students with a basic understanding of the library so that materials and time may be used efficiently when doing library research.

SCOPE: To help students make efficient use of time and library materials by acquainting them with the physical orientation to the library, the Library of Congress classification scheme, subject headings, reference tools, periodical indexes and abstracts, government documents information retrieval, search strategy processes, and compiling and annotating bibliographies.

TEACHING STRATEGY:

The course will be taught by a reference librarian in the University Library in a five-week period, using lecture and workshop formats. Printed information sheets will accompany each class lecture and worksheets will be assigned after each lecture to be completed and handed in. These worksheets will cover the materials in the lectures.

COURSE REQUIREMENTS:

Completion of worksheets assigned in class, and completion of a fifteen-item bibliography.

EVALUATION:

Evaluation forms will be used at the end of the course.

COURSE OUTLINE

FIRST SESSION:

General introduction to the library, explanation of the course, pre-test, tour.

Objectives of first session: To have an overview of the course. To allow student to become familiar with the physical layout of the library and with the location of several services.

SECOND SESSION:

Library of Congress classification system, subject headings, the card catalog, theories of organization.

Objectives of second session: To help student understand the LC classification system, and how books are arranged and knowledge is organized. To familiarize user with subject headings, scope notes and catalog cards.

(Figure 6 continues on page 70.)

Figure 6 (cont'd)

THIRD SESSION:

Reference materials.

Objectives of third session: To familiarize student with the wide variety of reference books—encyclopedias, dictionaries, directories, almanacs, bibliographies. To show user how to use reference materials effectively.

FOURTH SESSION:

Periodical indexes and abstracts.

Objectives of fourth session: To familiarize student with the wide variety of indexes and abstracts and to differentiate between the two. To show user the subject appropriateness of several indexes and abstracts by the use of subject headings.

FIFTH SESSION:

Newspaper indexes and microfilm.

Objectives of fifth session: To familiarize student with microfilm, microfilm readers, and newspaper indexes. To show user how newspapers and their indexes are valuable sources of information.

SIXTH SESSION:

Government documents.

Objectives of sixth session: To familiarize student with the wide variety of documents available and how to access them through indexes.

SEVENTH SESSION:

The search strategy process and topic selection.

Objectives of seventh session: To demonstrate to the student how an organized process of search strategy can aid them in topic selection to locate pertinent material effectively and efficiently. To illustrate why topic definition is important in doing research.

EIGHTH SESSION:

Compiling bibliographies.

Objectives of eighth session: To familiarize student with the correct bibliographic forms for a variety of library material.

NINTH SESSION:

Annotating bibliographies.

Objectives of ninth session: To teach student how to annotate items in a bibliography for an "annotated bibliography."

Figure 6 (cont'd)

TENTH SESSION:

      Subject bibliographies.

      Objectives of tenth session: To teach student how to compile an effective subject bibliography. Examples of bibliographies will be given. Fifteen-item bibliography and all completed worksheets due.

Because of the nature of the class, students cannot miss more than two sessions; individual students must take the responsibility for completing any missed worksheets.

SAMPLE WORKSHEETS

Card Catalog Worksheet
Library Research, Second Session

Name: _____   Soc. Sec. No.: _____

I.   Under what subject heading in the card catalog would you look to find books on remedial reading?

       How did you identify the correct subject heading?

       Under what other subject headings in the card catalog could you look for related materials if you were doing a thorough search on the subject?

II.   You remember reading a book a few years ago entitled *Chariots of the Gods.* You don't remember the author. Under what subject headings would you look in the subject catalog to find other books on the same subject?

III.   On what floor and section of the library would you go to look for the book with the call number * G 540 V646?

IV.   Where would you find the Breed and Sniderman *Drama Criticism Index*?

(Figure 6 continues on page 72.)

Figure 6 (cont'd)

V. Give the editor or author, and title of a collection of plays owned by the library.

_____

_____

VI. Does the library own the written texts of the four Nixon-Kennedy television debates?

_____

VII. Does the library own any magazines devoted to the subject of alcoholism?

_____

If so, what are the titles?

_____

_____

_____

_____

Reference Materials Worksheet
Library Research, Third Session

Name: _____   Soc. Sec. No.: _____

I. What kind of information does the title page of a reference book give you?

_____

_____

_____

_____

II. What does the preface or introduction of a reference book usually include?

_____

_____

_____

_____

III. Select the type of reference book that you think would be most appropriate in locating the information sought below. You may choose more than one term and use a term more than once. Terms to choose from:
almanac, general encyclopedia, biographical dictionary, gazetteer, atlas, guide or manual, handbook, bibliography, directory, annual.

1. Information on a current political leader.

_____

2. The founding date of a city.

_____

3. Current information on population figures worldwide.

_____

Figure 6 (cont'd)

4. The geographical location of places mentioned in the Bible.

5. Where to find out what current materials are available on a research topic on a particular subject.

6. A comprehensive record for a field of research.

7. An aid in finding bibliographies and other reference materials on a given field.

8. A brief overview of a subject or well-known figure.

9. A listing of major corporations.

10. The cost of living for a given year.

IV. Find the information requested in the appropriate reference book. Books to choose from:
Columbia Lippincott Gazetteer of the World, World Almanac, International Encyclopedia of the Social Sciences, Statistical Abstract of the United States, Congressional Directory, Encyclopedia of Associations, Occupational Outlook Handbook, U.S. Government Manual, Acronyms and Initialisms Dictionary.

1. What are the major tenets of Marxism?

2. Where was Sam Stratton born?

3. What does MASH stand for?

4. What is the future for jobs in the field of education?

5. When was Albany founded?

6. What is the accident rate in the United States?

7. What is the capital of Turkey?

8. What association is concerned with business education for teachers?

9. In what agency is the Peace Corps now located?

10. Who is the U.S. ambassador to Iran?

Figure 7
SAMPLE ADVANCED COURSE

TOPICS IN ADVANCED LIBRARY RESEARCH

GOVERNMENT PUBLICATIONS (UNL 389)

Meeting Times: Mondays, Wednesdays 3:35-4:30 p.m.
Dates of course: September 8th-October 13th, 1981

Room: University Library, B14

Instructors: Suzanne Aiardo, Mark Yerburgh   Phone: 457-3347

Readings: Joe Morehead. *Introduction to United States Public
                Documents.* Littleton, Colorado: Libraries Unlimited, Inc.,
                1978.
                The basic text will be supplemented by periodical articles as
                listed in the course outline.

Credit: One unit, graded A-E, no prerequisites.

COURSE OBJECTIVE: To provide students with an awareness of the
publications available from the federal, state and international publishing
channels; to teach bibliographic search strategies by which these publications
can be found so that materials and time may be used efficiently when doing
library research.

SCOPE: To familiarize students with the government publications section of
the library by acquainting them with: the physical layout of the area; the
SUDOC classification scheme; indexing tools to federal legislation and
publications; organization of and access to state and international documents;
information retrieval; search strategy.

TEACHING STRATEGY: The course will be taught by librarians using both
lecture and workshop format. Readings will accompany class lectures.
Worksheets will be assigned to practice using the materials covered.

COURSE REQUIREMENTS: Completion of all worksheets; oral
presentations; final assignments will be examination of a selected agency's
publications and will include a written synopsis of the agency history and an
accompanying annotated bibliography of ten agency publications.

EVALUATION: Students are pre- and post-tested; statistics are kept on
individual and group growth; students complete a course evaluation form
during the last session of the course.

Figure 7 reprinted by permission of Suzanne Aiardo.

Figure 7 (cont'd)

COURSE OUTLINE

FIRST SESSION: Overview; describe course and explain course objectives; hand out syllabus and reading assignments; provide general introduction to the library; review basic library skills and administer pre-test.

SECOND SESSION: Introduction to government documents; define "government document" and show examples of federal government documents; present historical outline of depository system and its implementation at SUNYA; explain SUDOC system; tour government publications area.

THIRD SESSION: Federal government publications; access through the *Monthly Catalog*; historical overview of access prior to 1895; comparison of *Monthly Catalog* format pre- and post-1976; READEX microprint; commercial indexes.

FOURTH SESSION: Statistical sources; census materials; *American Statistics Index*; *Statistical Abstract of the United States*; *Historical Statistics of the United States, Colonial Times to 1970*.

FIFTH SESSION: The legislative process, introduction; examine the bill process; trace and show samples of committee hearings, prints, House and Senate reports; examine finding tools, for example, *Congressional Information Service/Index, Commerce Clearinghouse Congressional Index, Congressional Record, Digest of Public General Bills and Resolutions, CQ Almanac, U.S. Statutes at Large, U.S. Code, U.S. Code Congressional and Administrative News*.

SIXTH SESSION: The legislative process, continuation with a legislative laboratory; followup to previous session by having each student choose a topic from a preselected list and trace a piece of legislation through its history.

SEVENTH SESSION: Administrative organization; introduction to department and agency publications; *Federal Register/Code of Federal Regulations, U.S. Government Manual*; examination of agency publications, annual reports, bibliographies, series, and periodicals.

EIGHTH SESSION: Report literature and library technology; *National Technical Information Service* (NTIS), *Resources in Education* (ERIC), *Government Reports Announcement and Index*; online demonstration of information retrieval.

NINTH SESSION: State documents; focus on New York state; access and organization; legislative, administrative, statistical sources.

TENTH SESSION: International documents; *United Nations Yearbook, UN Monthly Chronicle, Public Affairs Information Service* (PAIS); individual assignments due; post-test; evaluation.

Figure 8
SAMPLE FORM FOR LIBRARY ORIENTATION
AND INSTRUCTION REQUEST

(Please return to Anne Roberts, Library 104, or call 457-3347; plan to discuss class visits or library instruction sessions at least one week before you wish the instruction to take place.)

Name of Instructor _____

Campus Address _____

Campus Phone _____ Home Phone _____

Name and Number of Course _____

Day and Time of Meeting _____

Library orientation and instruction may be tailored to meet the needs of the class; e.g., one session may include a general physical orientation to the library with a brief demonstration of how to use the card catalog and reference materials; another session may include a brief demonstration of periodical newspaper indexes and how to locate periodical or newspaper articles and an introduction to government documents and microforms.

What would you like included in the library instruction session?

1.	_____ Card Catalog	4.	_____ Government Documents
2.	_____ Reference Materials	5.	_____ Microforms
3.	_____ Periodical Indexes	6.	_____ Other (Specify)

Students find library orientation and instruction to be most useful when it is related to an assignment that requires them to use the library soon after their library instruction sessions in the library.

After their library instruction sessions, your students will have to:

1.	_____ Prepare a speech	4.	_____ Write a research paper
2.	_____ Prepare a bibliography	5.	_____ Find critical material
3.	_____ Write a short paper	6.	_____ Other (Specify)

When do you wish to bring your students to the library? (Please give an alternative date.)

_____

Do you wish more than one library instruction session?

_____

If so, how many, and for what purposes?

_____
_____
_____

(Please don't forget to fill out this form and return it as soon as possible to Anne Roberts, Library 104. The calendar fills up quickly.)

Figure 9
POINT-OF-USE: THE CARD CATALOG

The library houses close to a million catalogued volumes in open stacks on the four floors of the main library building. Subsidiary collections are found in several other areas. One is the branch library at the downtown campus near Draper Hall. This has materials related to education and social sciences. Another is the Library School Library which has specially related materials such as library literature and children's literature, including an historical children's collection. To provide maximum ease and speed of access would be an impossible task without a general reference tool available to all users. The primary reference tool in the library is the card catalog. The card catalog functions as a multiple access tool to most material found in the library. It is a large, descriptive, alphabetical index on typed or printed 3x5 cards. Not all materials are listed in the card catalog. Books, periodical titles, and on-order or received book slips for uncatalogued materials are available through the card catalog. Most government documents, individual periodical articles, and separate items of anthologies are not listed in the card catalog. Alternate access to these excluded materials is found in a wide variety of sources such as indexes and abstracts to periodicals, microfilms, and government documents. Even anthologies have specific contents indexes.

The main library catalog contains over three million cards, several of which refer to the same publication. All cards give the same kind of basic information in the same order and format. The card catalog is designed and maintained to facilitate searching procedures in many ways. One of these ways is by giving it two major divisions. The first one is the author/title catalog section, which is used if either the author or the title is known. The second division is the subject catalog, which gives another topical approach to materials if only the subject is known. Once you determine which catalog division is suited to your purpose, the labels on the individual drawers will further alphabetically subdivide the range indicated for the cabinet. The first and last cards of the drawer are indicated by the letters of the alphabet given on the label. For correct alphabetical access, there are several helpful rules for you to keep in mind. Word-by-word filing as contrasted by letter-by-letter filing is used in our catalog, and follows one word all the way through before starting the next. Drop the apostrophe and consider the "s" as part of the whole word alphabetically. The articles "a," "an," and "the" are ignored for alphabetic filing when any of them occurs as the first word of a title. Abbreviations and numbers are filed in order alphabetically as if spelled out. Words beginning with "M" or "Mc" are all filed as if they were spelled "Mac." The inside of the drawer often contains several tab cards which are raised above the rest of the cards for easy visibility. These tab cards show what the cards directly behind them begin with in the alphabet, and can thus narrow your search. In the author/title catalog, on what are generally called "main entry" cards, the author's name appears in bold black type filed alphabetically, last name first. This entry is the one that extends for the intellectual content of a work and may be an individual, several individuals, or a corporate body such as an institution or an organization.

(Figure 9 continues on page 78.)

Figure 9 (cont'd)

A title card is a duplicate of the author card except that the title appears at the top of the card as well as in the body. Occasionally there is not an author card, and then the title will be found only once as the main entry. Other parts of a catalog card carry additional bits of information that may be helpful when screening and selecting books for your research. Place of publication, publisher, and date can indicate currency, possible bias, or even authority. A date preceded by a "c" indicates the book's copyright; otherwise the date is the book's publication date. This short section, called the collation, gives the number of pages of introductory material, the total number of pages or volumes, and tells whether or not there are illustrations, maps, or other graphic material. The collation also tells the size of the book and whether or not the book is part of a series, which may be important. Another section of notes is occasionally included for a bibliography, an appendix, an alternate title, or specific contents of the material. An important part of the card is the section which lists subject headings for every topic fully discussed in the book. Cards carrying these are filed in a subject catalog and are separate from the author/title cards in the library. Some libraries have all three types of catalog cards filed in one card catalog; this is called a "dictionary card catalog." Subject catalog cards are identical to other cards except that the subject heading appears at the top of the card in red type or in all capital letters. Subjects or subject headings that are assigned to particular books appear at the bottom of the card. Here they are preceded by Arabic numerals, which are called tracings. These tracings, or subject headings, indicate all the subjects under which that particular book will be listed in the subject catalog within the card catalog. Each book may have many different subject headings, and each subject heading can cover many different books. If you are uncertain about a correct subject heading, or you are unable to find a topic in the catalog, check the two red volumes of the *Library of Congress Subject Headings* list. These are used to assign subject headings and will tell you which headings are used for subjects and which ones are not used. The symbols used in this list to express a subject heading are: an "sa" or see also, which points out the most closely related heading; an "xx," which means a less related heading; an "x," which refers back to the main heading in bold black type and therefore is not used as a heading itself; and a "-," which indicates that it is part of the main heading. The tracings at the bottom of the catalog card also include added entries. These are designated by Roman numerals and include titles, series, other contributors, illustrators, or joint authors. These entries will also have separate cards filed in the author/title section of the card catalog under the appropriate heading. Extraneous material, which is generally used internally by librarians within the library, can usually be ignored by you, the user.

Once you have found the books you want from the author/title subject cards, you are close to finding your material. The "call number," a combination of letters and numbers placed in the upper left-hand corner of the catalog card, indicates the specific location in the library where the particular book should be found. Special abbreviations found above the standard Library of Congress call number may provide additional information for locating the books. "LIB" indicates location in the Library School Library; "EXT" means the book is in the branch library; and "PER" tells you that the material is in the periodical room of the main library. "REF" means that the book is in the non-circulating reference collection, and an asterisk "*"

Figure 9 (cont'd)

indicates that the book is shelved in the oversize area of the main library. Other abbreviations that are given may be interpreted by consulting either the library directory or a reference librarian. Once the call number has been completely copied down, the library directory which gives locations should be consulted. Here the location of the call number is explained topically, and the proper floor is designated by using the first letter of the call number as its location key. On each floor a directory is located on the stairwell landing, giving the general arrangement of the books on each floor and call number designations.

When you arrive at the appropriate section of the library stacks, the stack end labels give you the call number range held by those shelves in that particular stack and you can now locate your books. The spine labels on a book will correspond exactly to the call number found on the card for the particular book you want. The library is an open stack library, so you must be able to use the card catalog to find the books you want. The card catalog is a complex tool; if you need help with it, the reference librarians are ready to help you.

Figure 10
SAMPLING OF A LIBRARY SKILLS WORKBOOK

THE BARE BONES OF BIBLIOGRAPHIC
BASICS: LIBRARY SKILLS

This workbook has been compiled by some of us in the library who want to help you find your way around the stacks and to help you get to use, know, and love some important library tools such as the card catalog, encyclopedias, dictionaries, indexes and abstracts, newspaper indexes, book review sources, and government documents, which will help you find information in the library.

Libraries, particularly large academic ones, are confusing places. Libraries are organized differently than other institutions, and they have their own peculiar systems for organizing and arranging materials. To compound the confusion, more and more published material is coming out every year and it is very difficult to keep track of all this new information, let alone the old. Libraries are always changing and things get moved around, which helps add to the confusion.

Before you begin this workbook, you should have taken the *Self-Guided Tour*, which will familiarize you with the physical setting of the library and with some of the services it provides. The workbook covers the most important aspects of library research which we feel you should know about in order to use the library effectively and efficiently.

Each section of the workbook explains the aspect we want you to cover, and then contains a brief exercise for you to do *after* reading the explanation. When you have completed the workbook, turn it in to the librarian you are assigned to. The workbook will be checked and then returned to you for you to keep.

(Figure 10 continues on page 80.)

Figure 10 (cont'd)

If you have any questions or problems along the way, please ask at the reference desk. We have arranged the order of the sections in the way that we think is the most logical one to gather information in order to give you an organized path to follow, or a search strategy, in doing library research.

Anne Roberts, Library Instruction Coordinator

TOPICS COVERED IN THE WORKBOOK INCLUDE THE FOLLOWING IN ORDER:

Dictionaries, Encyclopedias, Card Catalog—Author-Title Approach, Card Catalog—Subject Approach, Card Catalog—Locations, Periodicals and Periodical Indexes, Newspapers, Microforms, Almanacs and Statistical Sources, Biography, Book Review Sources, Government Documents, Information Retrieval, Appendix of Useful Information.

CARD CATALOG—LOCATIONS

We're almost finished with the card catalog. Just one last point of interest, which happens to be one of the most important pieces of information that you will find in the card catalog, and that is the call number. The call number, located at the top left-hand corner of the catalog card, indicates the specific location of a book in any library. It is made up of letters and numbers in a combination designated by the Library of Congress (LC) classification scheme, which the University Library uses for organizing and shelving its books. (Some libraries use the Dewey classification scheme.)

The first line of a call number refers to the broad class that the book is assigned to. It also provides a location key. Books with call numbers beginning with A through K are shelved on the third floor, and books with call numbers beginning with L through Z are shelved on the second floor.

There is a locational directory in the main lobby of the library that will enable you to translate your call number into a specific location. Additional directions are attached to the wall in each stairwell of the main library. These directions, along with maps, show the general location of books shelved on the respective levels. If the call number has a prefix such as REF, SPE, EXT, FIC, or CAS, this identifies the book as being in a special location. Again, consult the directory; it will direct you to the appropriate area.

Some of the books in the library are shelved in designated areas. The materials shelved in these areas are color coded and the catalog cards for these materials have colored plastic covers which correspond to the colored tape on the spine of the books:

Red means that the book is shelved in the law area;
Blue means that the book is shelved in the ready reference area;
Green means that the book is shelved in the government documents;
Black means that the book is shelved in the abstracts and indexes.

Books are arranged on the shelves in LC call number order. Always begin by locating the letters on the top line, using the first letter as a guide to the general

Figure 10 (cont'd)

area. The second line of the call number is a whole number, whereas the numbers following letters on the third and fourth lines are read as decimals. Here is an example:

L	L	LA	LB	LD
7	7	96	3063	4801
D47	D5	G5	R71	R19

If the book you are searching for is not on the shelf, consult with the circulation department at the circulation desk. The library has an automated online circulation system which can tell you where the book is.

Now you are ready to complete the exercise on the following page; you may refer back to this page if you get confused.

EXERCISE FOR CARD CATALOG – LOCATIONS IN WORKBOOK

Use the location directory in the library to answer questions 1 and 2:

1. The call number for *English Elements in Jonson's Early Comedy* is PR 2636 B22 1967. You can expect to find it:
    a. on the basement level
    b. on the second floor
    c. on the third floor

2. The call number for *Addresses to the People of Missouri* is SPE T 825 F3 M576x. You can expect to find it:
    a. on the basement level
    b. on the first floor
    c. in the reference area

3. Which of the following sets of call numbers is in correct order:

    a.
AI	AI	AI
3	9	9
E85	E9	G 4

    b.
HG	HG	HG
201	21	21
A7	A72	A8

    c.
LB	LB	LC
9	9	15
W5	W45	D25

To remember: Make sure you have all of the call numbers for the books on your topic and make sure of their location. If you cannot find the specific books on the shelves, consult with the circulation desk.

SUGGESTED ASSIGNMENTS

1. Prepare a point-of-use guide for a particular library tool. Good suggestions are: dictionaries; indexes; abstracts; maps or atlases; and the vertical file. Remember that this guide will be used independently of any library.

2. Write up a search strategy for a particular field of knowledge or subject discipline. Begin with a general overview from an encyclopedia; move on to appropriate subject headings and examples for both books and journal articles; note any specific tools of particular relevance for your search strategy.

SUGGESTED READINGS

Cook, Margaret. *The New Library Key.* New York: Wilson, 1975.

Downs, Robert B., and Clara O. Keller. *How to Do Library Research.* Urbana, IL: University of Illinois Press, 1975.

Dudley, Miriam. *Library Instruction Workbook.* Los Angeles: College Library, UCLA, 1981.

Freides, Thelma. *Literature and Bibliography of the Social Sciences: A Guide to Search and Retrieval.* Los Angeles: Melville, 1973.

Gates, Jean K. *Guide to the Use of Books and Libraries.* New York: McGraw-Hill, 1979.

Gore, Daniel. *Bibliography for Beginners.* New York: Appleton, 1973.

Kennedy, James R. "Integrated Library Instruction." *Library Journal* 95 (April 15, 1970): 1450-53.

Kennedy, James R.; Thomas G. Kirk; and Gwendolyn Weaver. "Course-Related Library Instruction: A Case Study of the English and Biology Departments at Earlham College." *Drexel Library Quarterly* 7 (1971): 277-97.

Phipps, Shelley E. "Why Use Workbooks? Or Why Do the Chickens Cross the Road? And Other Metaphors, Mixed." *Drexel Library Quarterly* 16 (1980): 41-53.

Renford, Beverly L. "A Self-Paced Workbook Program for Beginning College Students." *Journal of Academic Librarianship* 4 (September 1978): 200-205.

Roberts, Anne F. *The Bare Bones of Bibliographic Basics.* Albany, NY: SUNYA, 1979.

Roberts, Anne F. *A Study of Ten SUNY Campuses Offering an Undergraduate Credit Course in Library Instruction.* ERIC Document 157129, 1978.

Rogers, Sharon J. "Research Strategies: Bibliographic Instruction for Undergraduates." *Library Trends* 29 (Summer 1980): 69-81.

Stoffle, Carla J., and Judith M. Pryor. "Competency-Based Education and Library Instruction." *Library Trends* 29 (Summer 1980): 55-67.

Toy, Beverly M. *Library Instruction at the University of California: Formal Courses.* ERIC Document 116649, 1975.

Vuturo, Robert. "Beyond the Library Tour: Those Who Can, Must Teach." *Wilson Library Bulletin* 51 (May 1977): 736-40.

V

MEASURING THE RESULTS

TESTS AND TESTING

Instruction librarians, along with other teachers and educators, like to test. By giving tests, librarians feel they are doing the right thing and can add more data to their library instruction programs as test scores improve. Tests can be used in various ways: to capture the attention of library users, to identify attitudes about the library, to demonstrate what library users do or do not know, and to show whether or not the objectives of the library instruction skills are being understood or learned by the users. Also, from the users' point of view, a test can consolidate and reinforce their understanding of what has been learned.

To construct a reliable testing instrument is difficult since other factors enter into a test besides the items being tested. Maturity is one variable which enters into test construction, since library users familiar with other systems and drawing from more varied experiences may understand libraries better. Among the types of tests used in psychology and education are: norm-referenced tests (students are compared to each other on a relative scale), criterion-referenced tests (students are judged on an absolute scale), and semantic-differential tests (students are given a concept with a choice of words to select from). One of the biggest problems in the area of testing is in giving good directions to the test takers. Writing clear, objective, simple, and understandable directions is not an easy task; directions should be tried out on individuals who know nothing about what is being tested to see if they are clear and understandable.

Experts in the fields of psychological and educational testing emphasize that tests should be used to help students in evaluating their grasp of concepts and skills, not in evaluating their performance or knowledge of particular tools. In structuring tests, the test items should relate to the objectives that have been designed for the instruction that is being tested. One way of validating this process is to write objectives from the constructed test. Testing experts maintain that essay tests are best for testing concepts and comprehension, and that objective or short-answer tests do not really measure anything.

Library definitions, abbreviations, terms, and individual reference tools are the usual focus of library instruction tests. For most people, however, using a library for basic functions does not require that they know the meanings of library terms and library abbreviations, the "library lingo." Library users need to know the procedures for locating books, checking them out, initiating an interlibrary loan, and what questions to ask of librarians to help them in their search for information. Concepts may be what is most important for instruction librarians to teach their users. Less useful are specific definitions for words such as "annotation," "anthology," "bibliography," and "serial," and classification scheme outlines for Dewey and Library of Congress that are memorized for testing purposes. These have little meaning for users.

Too often instruction librarians use available tests for reasons of expediency, although these tests may bear little relationship to the library skills being taught. If instruction librarians are going to test, it is better for them to construct individual tests based on their own teaching objectives. Otherwise the test may act only as another barrier between the library and its users. Figure 11 (see p. 86) is an example of a library skills test that reflects the approach of one instructor-librarian. The test should grow out of individual approaches and take into account particular library conditions.

EVALUATING

There is general agreement among those in the library instruction field that evaluation methods and techniques that can better measure the performance of users and the effectiveness of library instruction programs are needed. Evaluation methods and techniques which have been used in library instruction, such as pre-tests and post-tests, or observations and surveys, have often been anecdotal and not particularly effective. All the known evidence in the area of evaluation indicates that library instruction may help users feel better about themselves, and this is a positive achievement. It means that library instruction can change, and change for the better, the affective behavior of users.

It is important to know what to evaluate, how to evaluate, and when to evaluate, for evaluation can help library instruction programs in several ways: it can measure the goals and objectives; it can determine the value of a program; and it can save time, effort, and resources by showing instruction librarians which elements are the most useful. Evaluation in library instruction is not highly developed, and there is no model for evaluation techniques. Two types of evaluation are used in library instruction: summative—done at the end of the library instruction activities; and formative or illuminative—done while the library instruction activities are being carried out. It is useful to employ both kinds of evaluation in library instruction, and most instruction librarians do, perhaps without even knowing it—for when a library instruction session or activity is going badly, most instruction librarians informally evaluate and change their approach.

Evaluation is really trying to find out what worked and why; the professional librarians want proof of their practices. A model that might be used profitably for instruction librarians in doing evaluation is one of evaluative research which is based on the scientific method and does the following:

1. Measures specific activities within the program first.
2. Defines the objectives and methods of the program clearly.
3. Applies experimental methods to the program.
4. Uses experimental and control groups in the evaluation.

One of the biggest problems with evaluation is that the traditional ways of carrying out programs are examined rather than the newly developing ones. Another problem is that activities tend to be counted and described rather than examined for their effectiveness; the quantity is emphasized over the quality. Too many of the objectives for most programs are based on common sense rather than on proven effectiveness; the levels of objectives are often confused, and too many of the objectives tend to be idealistic rather than realistic in many library instruction programs.

Other problems with methods of evaluation include: reliance on existing records and outdated information rather than generating accurate, current information; inadequate experimental designs with both control and comparison groups; failure to interpret the statistics collected, so that they have little meaning; and vague objective standards. Good evaluation requires time for planning, collecting information, and analyzing the information. The research design for an effective evaluative research measure contains: the statement of the problem with the formulation of the hypotheses; the collection and analysis of the data; and the measurement of the effect of the program. This last component requires that the measurement be both reliable and valid — difficult goals to accomplish. The best way to formulate evaluation methods is by building on the goals and objectives of the library instruction program. Assessing needs, determining goals and objectives, and evaluating and testing the results are all tied together.

Figure 11
SAMPLE LIBRARY SKILLS TEST

I. Arrange the following call numbers in the order you would expect to find the books so labeled on the library shelves.

A.	HF	B.	DA	C.	Z
	5838		4679		21
	D5		A9		B44
	1975		1958		1967

D.	DA	E.	HF	F.	HQ
	4697		5383		1426
	A76		D23		B69
			1972		

1. _____
2. _____
3. _____
4. _____
5. _____
6. _____

II. Arrange the following titles in the order in which you would expect them to appear in the card catalog.

A. *The Old Man and the Sea* 1._____
B. *To the Lighthouse* 2._____
C. *Operating Manual for Spaceship Earth* 3._____
D. *On the Experience of Time* 4._____
E. *Tortilla Flat* 5._____

Figure 11 (cont'd)

III. According to the following excerpt from *Library of Congress Subject Headings*, could you expect to find the subject heading "Photographic Wastes" in the Card Catalog?

> Photographic surveying *(TA593)*
>   *sa* Aerial photogrammetry
>   Photographic interpretation
>   *x*   Phototopography
>   *xx* Photogrammetric pictures
>   Photogrammetry
>   Photography—Scientific applications
>   Surveying
>   *Note under* Photogrammetry
>   —Mathematical models *(TA593)*
>   —Tables
> Photographic wastes
>   *See* Photography—Wastes, Recovery of
> Photographing of court proceedings
>   *See* Conduct of court proceedings
> Photographs
>   *sa* Aerial photographs

IV. Using the numbers that label the diagram below, identify the following parts of the catalog card:

    A. Call Number_____   C. Title_____
    B. Author_____   D. Publication Date_____
                             E. Publisher_____

   CT   Pirsig, Robert M.
   275   Zen and the art of motorcycle —5
1 < P468   maintenance: an inquiry into
   A33   values / by Robert M. Pirsig .--
           New York : Morrow, 1974. ﹨2
                    ﹨3   ﹨4

V. Using the numbers that label the diagram below, identify the following elements of the periodical index entry:

    A. Title of Article _____   D. Periodical Title _____
    B. Author _____   E. Volume Number _____
    C. Subject _____   F. Date of Issue _____

Women counselors
Female clients, female counselors: combating learned helplessness. M. Van Hook. Soc Work 24:63-5 Ja '79   1
2 **Women criminals**
New female criminal: reality or myth? C. Smart. bibl Brit J Criminol 19:50-9 Ja '79
Sex role sterotypes and justice for women. C. Feinman. Crime   3
    & Delinq 25:87-94 Ja '79
6 Valley of the bandit queens. N. K. Singh. Far E Econ R 103:32   4
    F 9 '79
5 Women and crime: an economic analysis. A. P. Bartel. bibl
    Econ Inquiry 17:29-51 Ja '79
Women geologists
Fear of frilly nighties; why are women barred from Britain's oilrigs? A. Coote. New Statesm 97:206 F 16 '79
More fear of frilly nighties [Great Britain]. A. Coote. New Statesm 97:251 F 23 '79
Women in agriculture
Land ownership and women's power in a midwestern farming community. S. Salamon and A. M. Keim. bibl J Marr & Fam 41:109-19 F '79

(Figure 11 continues on page 88.)

Figure 11 (cont'd)

VI.   In the following situations, *briefly* describe what steps you would take and what sources you would consult in the library to locate the information asked for.

     A.   Your psychology professor asks you to compile a list of twenty recent journal articles about the use of behavior modification with retarded children.

     B.   You are interested in learning more about passive solar heat and want to know if the U.S. government has any reports about its efficiency or plans for building a passive solar house.

     C.   Allen Ginsberg has been invited to give a poetry reading at the university. As a reporter for the *ASP*, you are assigned to write a biographical sketch of Ginsberg to appear in the newspaper the day before the reading.

     D.   For a paper about the recent political changes in Nicaragua, you want some information about the civil war that led up to the change in government.

SUGGESTED ASSIGNMENTS

1.   Devise a library skills test based upon objectives from your library instruction point-of-use guide or search strategy. This is good method to ensure that the objectives are realistic, obtainable, and measureable.

2.   Prepare an evaluation measure based on the objectives used in the exercise above; be sure to use the objectives in a way that they can be evaluated.

SUGGESTED READINGS

Hardesty, Larry; Nicholas P. Lovrich; and James Mannon. "Evaluating Library-Use Instruction. *College and Research Libraries* 40 (July 1979): 309-317.

King, David N., and John C. Ory. "Effects of Library Instruction on Student Research: A Case Study." *College and Research Libraries* 42 (January 1981): 31-41.

Lubans, John. "Mediated Instruction: An Overview with Emphasis on Evaluation." *Drexel Library Quarterly* 16 (January 1980): 27-40.

Nagy, Lasio A., and Martha Lou Thomas. "An Evaluation of the Teaching Effectiveness of Two Library Instructional Videotapes." *College and Research Libraries* 42 (January 1981): 26-30.

Paterson, Ellen P. "How Effective Is Library Instruction?" *RQ* 18 (Summer 1979): 376-77.

Person, Roland. "Long-Term Evaluation of Bibliographic Instruction: Lasting Encouragement." *College and Research Libraries* 42 (January 1981): 19-25.

Phillips, Linda L., and E. Ann Raup. "Comparing Methods for Teaching Use of Periodical Indexes." *Journal of Academic Librarianship* 4 (January 1979): 420-23.

Suchman, Edward Allen. *Evaluative Research.* New York: Russell Sage Foundation, 1967.

Tickton, Sidney G. *To Improve Learning.* New York: Bowker, 1970.

Tyler, Ralph. *Basic Principles of Curriculum and Instruction.* Chicago, IL: University of Chicago, 1950.

Vogel, J. Thomas. "A Critical Overview of the Evaluation of Library Instruction." *Drexel Library Quarterly* 8 (July 1972): 315-23.

Werking, Richard Hume. "Evaluating Bibliographic Education: A Review and Critique." *Library Trends* 29 (Summer 1980): 153-72.

Werking, Richard Hume. "The Place of Evaluation in Bibliographic Instruction." In *Proceedings of Southeastern Conference on Approaches to Bibliographic Instruction*, edited by Cerise Oberman-Soroka, pp. 100-118. Charleston, SC: College of Charleston, 1978.

VI
HANDLING THE COMPLEXITIES

DETERMINING NEEDS

There are many ways of determining goals and objectives for library instruction programs. Some instruction librarians have decided what it is their users should know; others have borrowed objectives from existing library skills programs and fitted them to their own needs, while others have surveyed their users to see what library skills users thought they needed.

An effective way to determine library instruction goals and objectives is through interviewing groups of users and compiling group profiles that cover a whole range of relevant characteristics: types of users (students, business workers, children, adults, retirees), place and type of residence, background, reasons for using the library, attitudes towards the library, past and present experiences with library instruction, expectations of the library, motivations for participating in library instruction programs, ways of carrying out the necessary library instruction for particular individuals or the group, and means of determining the successful completion of library instruction programs.

Other library staff members can be helpful to the library instruction program by participating in a needs assessment profile of library users; they might also be interested in having facts and statistics of their own for other library services such as circulation and interlibrary loan requests. The experiences of library staff members and their observations can provide different perspectives and even bring in new data about library user activity patterns and perceived needs.

Interviews allow for a more personal interaction than printed surveys or questionnaires. Face-to-face contact may elicit more information than might be received on a form, and the questions will usually be answered more thoughtfully and seriously than on a survey or questionnaire. The type of questions asked, particularly the open-ended ones, will yield much more information than closed questions which have set categories of answers. Sample interview questions include:

1. How would you evaluate your use of the library?

2. When do you need or like to use the library?

3. What skills do you wish you had to use the library?

4. What skills do you already have to use the library?

5. Who taught you those skills? Who can teach you more of them?

6. Do you like to find your own information?

7. Do you prefer someone else to find the information for you?

8. Which library do you like to use the most? Where is it?

9. Why do you like using this library the most?

10. How can the library staff be more helpful to you in your use of the library?

11. Should library skills be taught by the school, academic, or public library?

12. Should courses be offered through the library for research skills? Who should teach them?

By using the interviewing technique, instruction librarians can get a profile of users' needs to help them with their library instruction program objectives. Or the profile of users' needs may demonstrate that a library instruction program is not what is needed at all.

A needs assessment done by interviews may show what users want to know when they come to use the library: how to use the card catalog, especially the subject section; how to use journal indexes, particularly in subject fields; how to use government documents; how to select reference books in specific fields; how to outline search strategies that go beyond the card catalog; how to implement shortcuts and ways of summarizing information found in the library; how to evaluate sources of information; how to save time in doing library research; and how to be competent library users without the assistance of a librarian. What many needs assessment projects discover through the interview method is that most people feel uncomfortable in library situations that are unfamiliar to them. Even the most sophisticated library researchers are uneasy when they are doing research in a field not their own.

The findings of needs assessment surveys demonstrate that most library users like a wide variety of methods and techniques when they receive library instruction. Courses, mini-courses, course-related activities, tutorials, point-of-use instruction, audiovisual programs, and self-paced workbooks are some possibilities. Most users want to choose from a wide variety of formats so that they can feel comfortable while finding information. Users are sensitive to any overload of information; for example, those who are interested only in learning about the physical layout of the library do not also want to know how to use the card catalog at the same time. It is important to remember that what is familiar to the librarian is unfamiliar and often baffling to the user.

One result of doing a needs assessment project is the heightened awareness of the library by both librarians and users. The library staff may be brought together in the process of conducting a needs assessment survey in the search for common goals. This can be a significant staff morale booster, since all are working together to find out about users and their needs in the library. Even if it is decided that a library instruction program cannot be considered immediately, some useful information has been gathered, and the sheer act of going through the project together has allowed librarians and staff to work together in a joint effort. The information that is solicited by interviewing users is apt to be much more helpful and valid than that obtained by most surveys or questionnaires.

SETTING GOALS AND OBJECTIVES

Goals and objectives are important to library instruction; they should be realistic, attainable, appropriate, and consistent with the basic learning principles of readiness, motivation, and retention. They should be formulated to help answer the basic questions about setting up a library instruction program for the library: what are the roles of the users and the librarians in providing and supporting a library instruction program? should the library instruction program meet the immediate needs of users or develop the general long-range skills of library research and methodologies, or both? what are the most effective methods for teaching library skills for various levels of users in the library? and should the library instruction be attached to other activities or should it operate separately in the library? Determining the goals and objectives for a library instruction program is crucial for the formation of a solid enterprise. Goals and objectives can act as blueprints for a library instruction program as it is being established. Figure 12 (see p. 96) illustrates a set of goals and objectives for library instruction.

One educator, Ralph Tyler, defined educational objectives in terms of behavioral changes that occur when people learn. He believed that learning takes place when people acquire new behavior. For Tyler, behavioral objectives, as ways of thinking, feeling, and acting, can be generalized. Since behavior can be seen and is observable, it is a good measure for determining whether learning has occurred. Tyler posed these questions to define his educational objectives, expectations, or outcomes:

1. What educational purposes is the learning trying to accomplish?

2. What experiences are being provided to attain these purposes?

3. How can these experiences be effectively organized?

4. How can we determine whether or not these purposes are being attained?

Instruction librarians, recognizing that goals and objectives can help them in their programs, are asking the same questions. Goals and objectives can help librarians, they can help users, and they give users tangible expectations upon which the instruction is based. For instruction librarians, objectives help to select the content of the instruction, to motivate users, and to evaluate users and library instruction programs.

Goals and objectives in library instruction are generally on three levels: general, terminal, and enabling. General objectives describe the overall goals of the program and explain what the entire program is about. Terminal objectives separate the overall objectives into specific, meaningful units. Enabling objectives define the specific knowledge or skills necessary to achieve the terminal objectives. Examples of the three types of objectives are:

1. General: "The users will be able to use the library efficiently and effectively after completing the library instruction program."

2. Terminal: "Users view the library staff as sources of information."

3. Enabling: "The users ask the reference librarians for help when they are unable to answer library-related questions."

General and terminal objectives are relatively easy to write, while enabling objectives which describe the behavior instruction librarians want their users to acquire are more difficult. To help understand the enabling objective, it is useful to state the conditions under which users will demonstrate their behavior. Verbs which describe observable actions should be used to write enabling objectives: e.g., write, recite, identify, differentiate, solve, construct, list, ask, recall, complete, compare, contrast, distinguish, select, assign, describe, define, classify, and name.

The setting of goals and objectives is an essential component that must be mastered by instruction librarians. It may be easier to write goals and objectives for the program after some of the library instruction activities have been initiated, since they may then be easier to identify. Appendix C contains model objectives for library instruction.

ADMINISTERING, ORGANIZING, AND MANAGING THE PROGRAM

It has been suggested that the traditional organizational structures of libraries have not always been conducive to their functions of providing services and materials to users. This is particularly evident in the area of library instruction. One of the reasons given for the lack of support of library instruction over the years has been the lack of support on the part of library administrators. The programs that have been successful, it has been argued, are those that have had the complete backing of administrators.

Several library instruction proponents have moved into the field of administration and have suggested that library instruction requires a distinct type of management — one that fosters change. They maintain that when change and innovation occur, there is an increased likelihood that instruction librarians and instruction programs can become established. With the administration in favor of library instruction, optimum use is made of the library staff when it can be freed to do the important work of teaching users to use the library. Management style is a crucial element for the teaching library.

Organizing a library instruction program in an effective manner can be a key to getting needed administrative support. If the services of the library instruction program illustrate that the library provides its users with skills and materials they need, and demonstrate that the program is cost-effective, then administrative support may be strong. The ACRL Bibliographic Instruction Section, Continuing Education Committee, devised a series of checklists to be used at a preconference for beginning instruction librarians at ALA in Dallas, 1979 (see Appendix E). These twelve checklists for organizing and managing a library instruction program cover the components in a program for library instruction and include:

planning a model program, assessing needs, administering the program, writing objectives, developing materials, choosing modes and methods, teaching librarians to teach, determining management patterns, evaluating programs, and gaining support for the program. Basically, the checklists imply that there must be an impetus to begin a program or to revitalize an existing one; there must also be the feasibility of implementing a program. The library instruction program needs to be carried out by specified individuals, and with clear responsibility outlined for the liaisons with user groups. It is also important to determine responsibility for revising the instructional materials. Designated space and facilities are crucial if the library instruction program is going to succeed, and these arrangements also need to be worked out. Administrators want justifications and evaluations to make sure that programs are effective, and a carefully drawn-up organization plan can help provide these.

Libraries can be regarded as public organizations; they provide users with needed services and materials. Library instruction is one such service, and as with other organizations, there are several ways it can be provided: an "underground" instruction program in which librarians give instruction unofficially; approved programs in which one librarian gives instruction; programs given by subject specialists; and programs developed by all librarians but with one or two librarians coordinating the scheduling, and being responsible for teaching, record-keeping, and publicity.

PLANNING FOR LIBRARY INSTRUCTION

Planning is probably the most important element in getting ready for implementing a library instruction program. Assessing needs, determining goals and objectives, devising, evaluating, and testing procedures, choosing modes and methods and materials, and teaching procedures should all have been worked out. Only after this has been done can the proposed method of action be put into effect. The planning stage is one area where instruction librarians can benefit from some quiet time spent on thinking about the library instruction program and all of the activities and details that are involved. There are many parts to the planning step: analyzing the individual group targeted for the instruction in terms of numbers, ages, level of schooling, and areas of study; discussing activities with other interested people such as librarians, teachers, parents, students; reading about new methods, approaches, and materials; and going to professional meetings to gather ideas and suggestions from others in the field. The checklist in Figure 13 (see p. 97) delineates important factors in the planning process.

One of the important aspects of planning is to determine how the program will affect other areas of the library and other library services. It is important to include other library staff members as much as possible in the planning; asking for their opinions and for their help with the exercises or materials or with the actual activities can be beneficial. It is also important that your plans be announced. This can be done in a variety of ways: a large wall calendar in a central location marked with groups coming for library instruction sessions; a request form to be sent out; a telephone number of a contact person; or policies and procedures clearly written down and then distributed to the library staff. If any audiovisual equipment is to be used, it is essential that it be in working order and that a spare be available in case the equipment breaks down. Materials and additional supplies of handouts must be kept on hand and monitored for reprinting, revising, or updating. Storage space is necessary for planning instruction programs. It is a good idea to keep a log or diary of the library instruction activities; statistics can also be kept at the same time. Policies and procedures can be written with professional standards and guidelines in mind, such as the ACRL model in Appendices B and C.

A useful and practical means of creating interest and visibility is to form a local interest group for library instruction. Informal meetings can include sharing ideas and programs or solving instructional problems by working together. It is always a useful idea to keep copies of sample library instruction materials for reference and referral; a library instruction materials file can be put together in a file cabinet, with materials in categories according to type of tool, subject, or type of publication (guide, handbook, tour, bibliography, pathfinder, exercise, or test). A helpful way to let other library staff members know about the library instruction program and the planning is to enlist their help in collecting materials for the library instruction materials file. At various times during the year, displays of the materials can be arranged so that staff members may examine them; if their names appear as contributors, proponents for the library instruction program have been gained.

In the same way, local gatherings of interested librarians, teachers, and friends help to publicize the library instruction program and solicit ideas and gather advice from library staff members and colleagues. An afternoon spent discussing mutual problems in library instruction may be rewarding in contributing to planning the library instruction activities and programs. This method of involving others is also a way to build support for the library instruction program, for when people feel they have had a part in planning activities they are more willing to support them. It is also extremely helpful to have input from a network of interested librarians from other institutions when planning and implementing a library instruction program; they can provide support and encouragement as well as advice. The more time spent in planning a library instruction program, the more successful it will be, since all the variables will have been thought about, talked about, and written about.

Figure 12
SAMPLE GOALS AND OBJECTIVES

To provide library orientation and instruction to patrons of the University Library in order that they may make the most effective use of its collections and services is the overall goal of the library instruction unit. It will be accomplished by the following objectives:

1. To provide library orientation and instruction in several ways.

    a. Library orientation tours and instruction sessions are available to groups who wish to visit the library. These tours and sessions are conducted by the appropriate librarians or other library staff members.

    b. Course-related instruction is offered at both the undergraduate and graduate levels by the subject bibliographers, but the instruction librarians provide general library use tools and services for teaching techniques.

    c. A one-credit library research course is offered for five weeks of each semester and is graded on a pass/fail basis. The course is geared to undergraduate students and is designed to give students a basic understanding of library research methods, including kinds of sources available and appropriate processes or strategies for doing research.

2. To develop and make available print and nonprint materials to aid users in their research with the library collections.

3. To act as a clearinghouse and resource for information in the area of library instruction for users as well as librarians.

4. To act as a liaison with other departments in the library for orientation and instruction services.

Figure 13
PLANNING FOR LIBRARY INSTRUCTION

1. Think about the environment: the setting, the institution, the programs, the size, the resources, the profile of users; assess the library in terms of personnel and materials; discuss ideas for library instruction with administrators and colleagues; assess the needs of the library users; determine a target group; devise a program for them with activities; discuss proposed program with administrators and colleagues in terms of practicality and effectiveness; make final plans; collect sample materials of similar programs to save time.

2. Plan the library instruction program: write objectives; determine staff needs for carrying out the program; determine staff needs for supporting the program in terms of materials and training methods; determine any equipment needs and space; list materials to be prepared; develop a budget; devise a schedule and projected timetable for implementation of the program; develop evaluation procedures for the program.

3. Implement the library instruction program: publicize the program to library staff, users, other interested people, and administrators; prepare instructional materials for teaching methods such as printed guides, worksheets, evaluation forms, handouts, statistical forms, report forms, and media materials; test the program on a small group first as a pilot study.

4. Continue the library instruction program: keep statistics of library instruction program and target groups; enlist support of library colleagues; conduct evaluation studies of program; publicize results to colleagues and administrators; revise the objectives if necessary; revise library instruction program to keep interest and methods fresh and interesting.

5. Evaluate the library instruction program: expand the program if need is there and support is forthcoming; keep the program going for several years to examine effectiveness over a period of time; change the program as the users change.

Figure 13 adapted with permission from Carolyn Kirkendall.

SUGGESTED ASSIGNMENTS

1. Design a needs assessment instrument; it may be in the form of a checklist or a questionnaire. Assess the users in terms of age, educational level, geographical distribution, current use of the library, and any other variables that are appropriate.

2. Construct objectives for the library based upon the findings of the needs assessment. Write general, terminal, and enabling objectives for the library as a whole, and for one library instruction activity itself.

SUGGESTED READINGS

Association of College and Research Libraries, Bibliographic Instruction Section, Continuing Education Committee. *Organizing and Managing a Library Instruction Program.* Chicago, IL: American Library Association, 1979.

Best, John W. *Research in Education.* Englewood Cliffs, NJ: Prentice-Hall, 1970.

Boston, Robert E. *How to Write and Use Performance Objectives to Individualize Instruction.* Englewood Cliffs, NJ: Educational Technology Publishers, 1972.

Breivik, Patricia. "Leadership, Management, and the Teaching Library." *Library Journal* 103 (October 15, 1978): 2042-47.

Cottam, Keith. "An Instructional Development Model for Building Bibliographic Instruction Programs." In *Proceedings of the Southeastern Conference on Approaches to Bibliographic Instruction*, edited by Cerise Oberman-Soroka, pp. 33-40. Charleston, SC: College of Charleston, 1978.

Craig, Dorothy P. *Hip Pocket Guide to Planning and Evaluation.* Austin, TX: Learning Concepts, 1978.

Dillon, Howard W. "Organizing the Academic Library for Instruction." *Journal of Academic Librarianship* 1 (September 1975): 4-7.

Dyson, Allan J. "Organizing Undergraduate Library Instruction: The English and the American Experience." *Journal of Academic Librarianship* 1 (March 1975): 9-13.

Guskin, Alan E.; Carla J. Stoffle; and Joseph A. Boisse. "The Academic Library as a Teaching Library: A Role for the 1980s." *Library Trends* 28 (Fall 1979): 281-96.

Hennig, Margaret, and Anne Jardim. *Managerial Woman.* New York: Doubleday, 1977.

Jay, Anthony. *Management and Machiavelli.* New York: Bantam, 1967.

Kanter, Rosabeth Moss. *Men and Women of the Corporation.* New York: Basic Books, 1976.

Kirk, Thomas G. "Library Administrators and Instruction Librarians: Improving Relations." *Journal of Academic Librarianship* 6 (January 1981): 345.

Kirk, Thomas G.; James R. Kennedy, Jr.; and Nancy P. Van Zant. "Structuring Services and Facilities for Library Instruction." *Library Trends* 29 (Summer 1980): 39-53.

Lipsky, Michael. *Street Level Bureaucracy.* New York: Russell Sage, 1980.

Lossing, Sharon. "Reaching Graduate Students: Techniques and Administration." In *Faculty Involvement in Library Instruction*, edited by Hannelore B. Rader, pp. 75-96. Ann Arbor, MI: Pierian, 1976.

Mager, Robert F. *Preparing Instructional Objectives.* Belmont, CA: Fearon Publishers, 1975.

Robbins, Jane. "Reference Librarians: A Street Level Bureaucrat?" *Library Journal* 97 (April 15, 1972): 1389-92.

Spencer, Robert. "The Teaching Library." *Library Journal* 102 (Mary 15, 1978): 1021-24.

Stoffle, Carla J. "Focus on Objectives: A Workshop on Writing Objectives on Bibliographic Instruction Programs." In *Proceedings of Southeastern Conference on Approaches to Bibliographic Instruction*, edited by Cerise Oberman-Soroka, pp. 7-32. Charleston, SC: College of Charleston, 1978.

University of Texas, General Libraries. *A Comprehensive Program of User Education for the General Libraries. The University of Texas at Austin.* Austin: University of Texas, 1977.

University of Wisconsin-Parkside, Kenosha. *Bibliographic Instruction Program.* Kenosha: University of Wisconsin-Parkside, Library/Learning Center, 1978. ED 169890.

Vargas, Julie. *Writing Worthwhile Behavioral Objectives.* New York: Harper and Row, 1972.

VII
CATERING FOR THE UNUSUAL

SPECIAL USES AND USERS
OF LIBRARY INSTRUCTION

Library instruction can be implemented in ways that are appropriate for special groups of users. Many libraries employ their library instruction programs to teach new staff about the library. Students, clerks, and secretaries can also benefit from the library instruction activities and programs, not only as users of the library, but as employees. Library instruction activities and programs can either be used as they exist or geared especially to a particular group, with relevant examples demonstrated or explained. All supervisors working with practitioners trained in the field, particularly for staff development, can be advocates of library instruction. Designing programs that fit the needs of various community groups—such as young adults, nursery-age children, senior citizens, foreign adults, and groups with emotional, physical, or psychological difficulties—is an appropriate use of library instruction. The two largest groups that have used the library in this way are external degree students, mostly adults, and culturally unassimilated groups, especially open admissions students. Both of these nontraditional groups are interested in using the library for course assignments. Many of the existing approaches, such as the self-paced or self-directed workbooks, are appropriate for their library instruction, although small class meetings and discussions about particular tools or strategies are often more effective. Usually these groups are highly motivated and very responsive to the library instruction program.

For people less highly motivated, library instruction may proceed more readily with audiovisual methods such as videotaping. Several librarians have used videotaping to motivate groups by encouraging their involvement in the assignments. This approach rests on the simple but obvious fact that people's attention will not lag if their pictures are being taken, and when this is done by means of videotape they are certain to be involved. Rather than drifting mentally, individuals will want to be included and to participate.

Library instruction can be valuable for continuing education and staff development, both for the librarians presenting it and for the users receiving it. The research, preparation, and instruction that librarians undertake in teaching library use contribute to their being better and more effective librarians. Along with added confidence in themselves as professionals, librarians often gain new respect for librarianship. Also, they will add to what they know—to their expertise—as they prepare themselves for library instruction.

Library instruction programs that are designed for special users need to be relevant, practical, and scheduled at the appropriate time for user needs, just like library instruction programs for any other group. Depending upon the nature of the group, certain aspects of the library instruction may take longer to grasp or to complete, so the implementation of the library instruction program may differ slightly. Things to keep in mind for special users are: they may be sensitive to failure in the library; they are not likely to seek assistance from librarians; they want to go at their own pace; and they want to deal with materials that they can easily comprehend.

It is important to have empathy with whatever user group is being provided library instruction, but it is particularly important with users who have a language problem or who are physically handicapped. For example, foreign students, as a special users group, may not see the need for using libraries since they are accustomed to learning everything from teachers or textbooks. It is well to remember that these groups are not less intelligent than others; it is not necessary either to shout at them or repeat the same statement over and over.

Much attention has been paid to the culturally unassimilated, particularly in the 1960s because of open admissions to colleges and universities. Students learn from interacting with their environment, not just from formal instruction; they learn from their life situations, which may not be the same for all users. It is important for instruction librarians to be aware of both the strengths and the limitations of all groups. In working with groups of culturally unassimilated students, it is important to integrate them into college life so they are not so isolated and alienated. Once the skills are acquired, culturally disadvantaged students are able to succeed along with other students.

The principles remain the same for library instruction programs for special uses or for special users. Sensitivity to the needs of each situation is important. A successful learning environment requires that instruction librarians give the same care and attention to planning and implementing in all situations.

COMPUTERS AND LIBRARY INSTRUCTION

The present and future image of the librarian is one of the technologist or information specialist, and this role is appropriate when the librarian is the intermediary between users and some computerized library services such as online searching of subject data bases. But other computerized library services, such as circulation operations or computer-assisted instruction, are designed for users and do not always require librarians as intermediaries. Rather, they require librarians to be instructors, especially in the self-teaching and practical areas. Because most users are relatively sophisticated when it comes to computers and technology, it is the librarian's job, as educator, to foster self-reliance among them.

Many computerized circulation systems allow for direct user contact without using librarians as intermediaries. These systems are often self-instructional, and users are able to interact with them easily. Because of the exposure to computers in their personal lives, many users are as comfortable with computers in libraries as most librarians, and want practical experience using them. Most library instruction for using computers consists of giving publicity, information, and directions. Users want instruction librarians to define the systems, describe how they work, and give specific examples and procedures in using the library computers. As users become more familiar with computerized systems in libraries, it is essential for instruction librarians to distinguish one computerized system from another since not all computerized systems have the same capabilities.

Online searching of data bases is usually integrated with the rest of the library instruction program, since it is another way of conducting a search strategy for needed information. Figure 14 is a sample script which was written to accompany an audiovisual presentation to introduce computer searching. The concepts of data base searching work with the concepts of searching print indexes, particularly if the data base has its print counterpart. Users can make comparison searches with both the print and the online data base in the same subject areas. Libraries are becoming involved with online searching of periodical indexes, an area that is less costly than some of the other abstracting services. *Magazine Index, Monthly Catalog of Government Publications*, and *Science Citation Index* are good examples of periodical indexes which can be used effectively with their print counterparts without an enormous outlay of money. They can help users become proficient in using both computerized and print indexes. The search strategy can be used with more precision since users can immediately see their results with both print and computer searches.

In order to integrate computerized searching effectively into the library instruction program, certain requirements are necessary: a computer; the computer-assisted instruction language; computer personnel for consulting, programming, and training of librarians; good publicity; money for equipment and programs; and staff for training and teaching. With small home computers becoming so popular and familiar, libraries will become more involved in using computers for various aspects of their operations and services.

Computerized library instruction will undoubtedly become widespread as the costs go down and as computers become more common. Many users will own small home computers, like the APPLE, PET, TRS-80, OSBORNE, and the ATARI. The technology, which is changing so rapidly, will shape the teaching methods used in library instruction for acquiring library skills, particularly those that relate to using computerized systems in libraries.

THE FUTURE OF LIBRARY INSTRUCTION

Library instruction has a long history, and within the last two decades, it has been an active one. Many of its proponents view library instruction as a professional discipline since it fulfills the requirements of a profession: library instruction possesses a distinct and defined body of knowledge with a broad intellectual base; it has self-initiated research and study programs carried on by its members to extend that specialized body of knowledge; and it provides service to individuals and to society. The element lacking in library instruction to qualify it as a profession is precise standards for admission and practice which are established and enforced by the members acting as a body through a professional organization. Several professional organizations are addressing the question of standards.

Library instruction has come of age, but many problems remain unresolved. Immediate concerns are: the integration of library instruction into the library profession; the integration of library instruction into higher education; the integration of library instruction into library schools; the integration of library instruction into concepts of learning and into technology; the integration of library instruction into professional research; and the integration of library instruction into the literature of the profession.

Some future trends within library instruction can be predicted: library instruction will be considered a standard library service; instruction librarians will work closely with library schools, in both teaching and research; they will look carefully at the history of librarianship and the place of instruction within it, perhaps even rewriting the history; they will work together in integrating materials and methods of their programs; they will implement their programs within educational frameworks; they will carry out ethnographic and behavioral studies of users, particularly in the fields of reading and writing; they will develop solid evaluation methods for their programs; and they will focus on individual learners and learning styles as well as the effect of information on learners in relationship to their instruction programs.

Instruction librarians have traditionally been agents of change, and this will no doubt continue as libraries respond to the changes in society which will affect libraries and librarians. Instruction librarians will move into the arena of holistic librarianship, paying attention to the mental, physical, emotional, and spiritual aspects of users as they seek information in libraries.

Figure 14
SAMPLE INTRODUCTION FOR COMPUTER SEARCHING

THE INFORMATION RETRIEVAL SCRIPT

The university library offers a number of services which are available to you for your research. One of these is the computer-based reference service offered through the information retrieval section of the library. Have you checked the appropriate print indexes in the library's reference area and been unable to find the material which is relevant to your needs? Working on a new concept that hasn't yet been assigned a subject heading? Doing a dissertation or research project for which you need a really comprehensive literature search? Trying to find articles that combine the interaction of several variables? Then perhaps you can use the computer to help you solve your library research problems. To find out more about the computer search service available at the library, ask for an informational leaflet at the reference desk, or, if you already have a good idea of your research problem, make an appointment for a search at the information retrieval section or the reference desk. Your appointment will take approximately 30 minutes of your time. Before you come to the appointment, you will be asked to complete a search request form. This saves time during your interview with the search analyst, and also allows you to limit your research problem beforehand. In some areas you will have the option of limiting your search to articles published only in

(Figure 14 continues on page 104.)

Figure 14 reprinted by permission of Sara D. Knapp.

Figure 14 (cont'd)

the English language, or to specify those other languages with which you are familiar.

When you make an appointment for a search, a database will be chosen for you which corresponds to the subject area of your work. The databases are stored on magnetic tapes, which include the necessary publication information and subject headings under which articles and reports are indexed. These tapes, which the computer is able to "read," are called "databases." Each database is loaded into a computer system which allows conversational searching through the use of a computer terminal. From time to time, new databases are added to the files of the system. Currently we are in the Biomedical Communication Network (BCN), which includes university, medical, and special libraries located from Boston in the east to Minneapolis in the west and as far south as Richmond. At present the network's files include four databases which correspond to print indexes with which you may already be familiar. These are: the *MEDLARS* database, which covers *Index Medicus, International Index to Nursing Literature*, and *Index to Dental Literature*, and goes back as far as 1964; the *Psychological Abstracts* database, which corresponds to the print *Psychological Abstracts*, and can be searched as far back as 1967; the *ERIC* database, which includes two print indexes — *Research in Education* back to 1966 and *Current Index to Journals in Education*, which is searchable back to its beginning in 1969; the *Biological Abstracts* database, corresponding to *BA Previews*, and covering *Biological Abstracts* and *Bioresearch Index* and searchable back to 1973. The material on the databases is not restricted to fields of medicine, biology, psychology, and education, but also includes much from allied fields such as biophysics, chemistry, counseling, nursing, rehabilitation, environmental sciences, reading, administration, library science, and many other subjects.

When you come to the information retrieval area for your appointment the search analyst will use your completed form of the search request in an interview with you designed to help gain a good understanding of your search needs. This search request will then be translated into a formulation or logical statement of key words, subject headings, and other codes which describe the type of articles you are seeking in the language of the computer. This formulation will be tried out at the computer terminal, which looks very much like a typewriter. A sample of titles will be retrieved for examination for relevance. If the original formulation is found to be unsatisfactory, the search analyst will modify the formulation. Your cooperation is essential in this process, and you will be asked whether the sample of titles and number of articles are satisfactory for your purposes. When you and the search analyst have arrived at a mutually satisfactory statement of your search, it will be printed, The printing will be done offline and sent back to the library — an activity that takes about four or five days. The final printout will include full citations for reports or articles and the abstract number in the print indexes. Abstracts will be included only if they are unavailable in print form at the university library.

To determine whether or not the materials you want are located in the library, consult the author/title catalog for titles of periodicals or books. Periodical holdings are listed in the periodical printout, copies of which are available in the reference section, the government publications area, and the periodical room. For ERIC documents, you should consult the ERIC

Figure 14 (cont'd)

microfiche files, which are in the government publications area. For materials which are not available in the library, consult the interlibrary loan office. The computer is useful in helping patrons obtain current information that may not yet have appeared in subject headings in the printed indexes, so the interlibrary loan help can be useful.

The computer is helpful in locating information on topics which are so specialized that much time would have to be spent in searching through printed indexes and abstracts for just the right material. The information retrieval section of the university library provides one method by which modern technology can be utilized to improve library service. If you have any questions about this process, please ask a reference librarian for clarification.

SUGGESTED ASSIGNMENT

1. Prepare a library instruction session for library users. Use the class or colleagues as users. The session may be on a library tool, concept, service, or research strategy. Write objectives, design any handouts, and outline any talk or speech you are giving if these items are to be included in your session. Ask for critiques and evaluations.

SUGGESTED READINGS

Bennis, Warren G. *The Planning of Change.* New York: Holt, Rinehart and Winston, 1971.

Berman, Louise. *New Priorities in the Curriculum.* Columbus, OH: Charles E. Merrill, 1968.

Bezugloff, Natahag. "Library Services to Non-English-Language Minorities in the United States." *Library Trends* 29 (Fall 1980): 259-74.

Biggs, Mary M. "On My Mind—The Perils of Library Instruction." *Journal of Academic Librarianship* 5 (July 1979): 159 + .

Boss, Richard W. "The Library as an Information Broker." In *New Horizons for Academic Libraries*, edited by Robert Stueart and Richard D. Johnson, pp. 43-49. New York: K. G. Saur, 1979.

Bradshaw, Charles I., and Marvin E. Wiggins. *Using the Library: The Card Catalog.* Provo, UT: Brigham Young University Press, 1971.

Breivik, Patricia Senn. *Open Admissions and the Academic Library.* Chicago, IL: American Library Association, 1977.

British Library Research and Development Reports. *Library User Education: Are New Approaches Needed?* London: British Library Board, 1980.

Carnegie Foundation for the Advancement of Teaching. *Missions of the College Curriculum*. San Francisco: Jossey-Bass, 1977.

Caruso, Elaine. *Computer Aids to Learning for Online Retrieval Systems*. Pittsburgh: Graduate School of Public and International Affairs, 1981.

Cashen, Carol J. "From Basic to Collegiate Skills." *Journal of Developmental and Remedial Education* 4 (Winter 1981): 22-24.

Cohen, David. "Ethnicity in Librarianship: A Rationale for Multiethnic Library Services in a Heterogeneous Society." *Library Trends* 29 (Fall 1980): 179-90.

Conroy, Barbara. *Library Staff Development and Continuing Education*. Littleton, CO: Libraries Unlimited, 1978.

Dickinson, Dennis W. "Library Literacy: Who? When? Where?" *Library Journal* 106 (April 15, 1981): 553-55.

Evans, Richard I. *Resistance to Innovation in Higher Education*. San Francisco: Jossey-Bass, 1968.

Furlong, Elizabeth J., and Karen J. Horney. "The Future in Our Grasp: An On-Line Total Integrated System for Library Service." In *New Horizons for Academic Libraries*, pp. 170-74. New York: K. G. Saur, 1979.

Hagemeyer, Alice. *The Public Library Talks to You*. Washington, DC: Gallaudet College Center for Continuing Education, 1975.

Haro, Robert P., "Academic Library Services for Mexican Americans." *College and Research Libraries* 34 (November 1972): 454-62.

Herndon, Gail A., and Noelle Van Pulis. "The On-Line Library: Problems and Prospects for User Education." In *New Horizons for Academic Libraries*, pp. 539-44. New York: K. G. Saur, 1979.

Knapp, Sara D. "Instructing Library Patrons about Online Reference Services." *Bookmark* 38 (Fall 1979): 237-42.

Lancaster, Frederick Wilfred. "User Education: The Next Major Thrust in Information Science?" *Journal of Education for Librarianship* 11 (Summer 1970): 55-63.

Learning Technology Incorporated. *Library Skills: A Program for Self-Instruction*. New York: McGraw-Hill, 1970.

Lee, Joann H., and Arthur H. Miller, Jr. "Introducing Online Data Base Searching in the Small Academic Library: A Model for Service without Charge to Undergraduates." *Journal of Academic Librarianship* 7 (March 1981): 14-22.

Lipow, Anne Grodzins. "Teaching the Faculty to Use the Library: A Successful Program of In-depth Seminars for University of California, Berkeley, Faculty." In *New Horizons for Academic Libraries*, pp. 262-67. New York: K. G. Saur, 1979.

Lolley, John L. *Your Library—What's in It for You?* New York: John Wiley and Sons, 1974.

McGinnis, Raymond G. *New Perspectives for Reference Service in Academic Libraries.* Westport, CT: Greenwood, 1978.

Nielsen, Brian. "Online Bibliographic Searching and the Deprofessionalization of Librarianship." *On-Line Review* 4 (Spring/Summer 1980): 215-24.

Rogers, Everett M. *Communication of Innovation.* New York: The Free Press, 1971.

Rosenblum, Joseph. "The Future of Reference Service: Death by Complexity." *Wilson Library Bulletin* 52 (December 1977): 300-301 +.

Schiller, Anita R. "Reference Service: Instruction or Information?" *The Library Quarterly* 35 (January 1965): 52-60.

Simsova, Sylvia. "Library Training for Services to Minority Ethnic Groups: Concepts and Principles." *Library Trends* 29 (Fall 1980): 245-58.

Wasserman, Paul. *The New Librarianship: A Challenge for Change.* New York: Bowker, 1972.

Wilson, Pauline. "Librarians as Teachers: The Study of an Organization Fiction." *Library Trends* 49 (April 1979): 146-62.

APPENDIX A
POLICY STATEMENT: INSTRUCTION
IN THE USE OF LIBRARIES

Utilization of information is basic to virtually every aspect of daily living in a democratic society, whether in the formal pursuit of educational goals or in independent judgment and decision making. In our post-industrial, increasingly complex society, the need for information daily becomes greater.

Libraries are a major source of information; however, their effective use requires an understanding of how information is organized and how individuals can retrieve that information. Many individuals have an inadequate understanding of how to determine the type of information needed, locate the appropriate information, and use it to their best advantage.

Instruction in the use of libraries should begin during childhood years and continue as a goal of the formal educational process in order to prepare individuals for the independent information retrieval essential to sustain life-long professional and personal growth.

It is essential that libraries of all types accept the responsibility of providing people with opportunities to understand the organization of information. The responsibility of educating users in successful information location demands the same administrative, funding, and staffing support as do more traditional library programs.

The American Library Association encourages all libraries to include instruction in the use of libraries as one of the primary goals of service.

American Library Association, Council Document #45, 1980. Reprinted by permission of the American Library Association.

APPENDIX B
TOWARD GUIDELINES FOR BIBLIOGRAPHIC INSTRUCTION IN ACADEMIC LIBRARIES

GUIDELINES FOR BIBLIOGRAPHIC INSTRUCTION IN ACADEMIC LIBRARIES

The Association of College and Research Libraries Bibliographic Instruction Task Force recognizes that it is a responsibility of an academic library not only to support the teaching function of its parent institution but also to actively participate in that function. A basic responsibility of an academic library is to instruct the community in the effective identification and use of information resources relevant to their needs and interests. To meet ACRL recognized standards of library service, each academic library shall provide an effective program of instruction to its community as one of its major public services. Effective instructional programs will be characterized by:

1. A written profile of the information needs of various segments of the academic community.

2. A written statement of objectives of instruction which:

    a. will include long-range and immediate goals with projected timetables for implementation.

    b. will be directed to specific identified needs within the academic community and make provisions for various methods of instruction to all segments of the academic community who have a need to use library facilities and services.

    c. outline methods by which progress toward the attainment of instructional objectives can be measured. Methodology must provide for measures of academic community learning, academic community attitudes, and cost effectiveness of instruction.

Reprinted by permission of the American Library Association from *College & Research Libraries News*, April 1977; copyright © 1977 by the American Library Association.

3. Continuing financial support:

   a. clearly identifiable within the library's budget programs and statements.

   b. sufficient to provide for the professional and supportive staff, equipment, materials, and facilities necessary to attain the delineated objectives.

4. Librarians and other qualified staff responsible for planning, implementing, and evaluating the program:

   a. inclusive of persons with training in: various academic disciplines, the identification and use of library resources, teaching skills, preparation and use of audiovisual and other teaching materials, preparation and use of evaluative instruments, clerical skills.

   b. in sufficient numbers necessary to attain the delineated objectives.

   c. clearly identifiable and of a status similar to persons responsible for planning, implementing, and evaluating the other major functions of the library.

5. Facilities, equipment, and materials available to accommodate the preparation of instructional materials and the presentation of various modes of instruction (individual, small group, large group, lecture, discussion, media, etc.); of sufficient number, size, and scope to accommodate the attainment of the delineated objectives.

6. Academic community and library community participation in the formulation of objectives and the evaluation of their attainment.

7. Attainment of written objectives for a five-year period.

The written statement of objectives identified in 2 is a significant element in an effective instructional program; *it of necessity must be unique to each institution and be the product of that institution.* The statement of objectives which the ACRL Bibliographic Instruction Task Force has prepared is appended and is intended to serve as a model which individual libraries should review and adopt to their purposes.

APPENDIX C
ACADEMIC BIBLIOGRAPHIC INSTRUCTION: MODEL STATEMENT OF OBJECTIVES

by ACRL Bibliographic Instruction Task Force*

While reviewing the model statement, a few points should be kept in mind:

1. The model statement's primary purposes are to (a) get academic librarians to focus on and articulate what their instructional objectives should be and to design instructional programs to achieve these objectives and (b) stimulate research into whether existing programs are achieving these objectives.

2. The objectives are those for an entire program of bibliographic instruction in an academic institution.

3. The objectives are intended to cover bibliographic instruction programs for *undergraduates.* Some objectives are no doubt applicable to any level of student, but these objectives in their totality are intended to speak specifically to the needs of undergraduates.

4. The objectives do not suggest one method of instruction nor should they be used for evaluating a particular instruction unit.

5. An attempt has been made to write the enabling objectives (E's) as *behavioral* objectives. In any institution's revision or individually written objectives, the objectives should be specific and measurable.

---

*Thomas Kirk, Elizabeth Butler, Joan R. Freudenthal, Stefania A. Koren, Anne B. Passarelli, Hannelore B. Rader, Dennis F. Robison, and Sara Lou Whildin.

Reprinted by permission of the American Library Association from the *Bibliographic Instruction Handbook*, by the Policy and Planning Committee, Bibliographic Instruction Section, Association of College and Research Libraries (Chicago: ACRL, 1977), pp. 36-45.

6. The arrangement of the terminal objectives and the related enabling objectives is not intended to suggest a sequence for an instructional program nor is it intended to suggest an order of significance. The task force has debated extensively whether the objectives should include aspects of what has commonly been called orientation in what is supposed to be a statement on bibliographic instruction. The task force is absolutely convinced that orientation is not sufficient, neither are we convinced that meaningful instruction can be divorced from orientation to a particular library.

7. The task force believes that the primary role of bibliographic instruction is to provide students with the specific skills needed to successfully complete their assignments. But in addition, bibliographic instruction should also serve the more general function of preparing students to make effective life-long use of the library regardless of specific course work. Individual librarians or library staffs must use all of their skills to develop an instruction program that achieves these or revised objectives in the context of the students' course and library use.

The model statement is composed of a series of terminal objectives (T1, T2, T3a, T3b, etc.) written during 1973. These objectives have received the careful attention of the task force and other librarians involved in library instruction. Since October 1973, the task force has been working on the enabling objectives (E1, E2, etc.) which are listed under each terminal objective. The final version was approved by the committee at its meeting during the American Library Association conference in July 1974. Modest changes were made during 1978 and 1979.

OBJECTIVES

General Objective: A student, by the time he or she completes a program of undergraduate studies, should be able to make efficient and effective use of the available library resources and personnel in the identification and procurement of material to meet an information need.

T1. The student recognizes the library as a primary source of recorded information.
   E1. When observed in real situations, students regularly turn to the library for needed information. These contacts include attempting to find information on their own using the appropriate library resources, and when that is not successful they contact a librarian.
T2. The student recognizes the library staff, particularly the reference staff, as a source of information, and is comfortable seeking assistance from staff members.
   E1. Given a map of the library, the student is able to locate key service points (e.g., circulation, reserve, periodicals). The student can identify the location of information and/or reference area(s) of the library.

E2. Given a list of materials with call numbers and/or location symbols, a student can successfully retrieve all materials in the library that are properly shelved.

E3. The student can identify the members of the reference staff by sight and locate their offices.

E4. (If applicable) the student can identify by name the member(s) of the reference staff best qualified to assist him in his subject major.

E5. The student asks the reference staff for assistance whenever library-related information is needed.

E6. When asked about library services, the vast majority of students will respond positively to questions such as: "Are there people within the library who are willing to give assistance in locating needed information?" "Do these people give competent assistance?"

T3. The student is familiar with (or he has knowledge of) the library resources that are available to him.

    a. The student knows what library units exist on his campus and where they are located. The student knows what major information resources and collections are available in these units.

E1. While seeking information from the library, students will use most campus library units which contain substantial material relevant to their topic.

E2. While using the library, students will use a variety of collections within the central library: documents, pamphlet file, microfilm, etc., as appropriate.

    b. The student understands the procedures established for using these facilities.

E1. A student can sign out a library item correctly (as defined by each institution).

E2. The student can interpret library forms (e.g., overdue notices, search forms, hold requests, etc.).

    c. The student knows about the off-campus information facilities available and how to approach their resources.

E1. A student will ask the reference staff for advice about the possibility of other information resources outside the "official libraries" of his college or university when those sources do not meet his needs.

E2. A student who has need of materials which the library does not have will request that they be borrowed from another library.

T4. The student can make effective use of the library resources available to him.

    a. He knows how to use institutional holdings records (such as the card catalog and serials holdings lists) to locate materials in the library system.

E1. Given a map of the library, the student can correctly identify the location of the library's catalog (e.g., card catalog, book catalog, public shelf list) and other holdings lists in a specified period of time.

E2. The student will correctly identify and explain the purpose of selected elements on a sample catalog entry in a specified period of time. The selected elements will include: the author, title, place of publication, publisher, date of publication, series title,* bibliographic notes, tracings, and call number.

E3.   Given a topic or list of topics, the student will accurately list items found in the library's catalog on those topics in a specified period of time. The topics will include items which require the student to use the U.S. Library of Congress *Subject Headings* to compile a list of relevant, related subject headings. The student will also have to demonstrate his knowledge of form subdivisions, and subject filing rules such as historical subdivisions are filed in chronological order.

E4.   Given a list of materials, the student, in a specified time, can correctly identify and locate those materials in the library's catalogs which the library owns. The list shall include incomplete citation, citations which are listed under entries other than the "main entry." It will also include:

        Book (individual author)
        Book (corporate or institutional author)
        Book (title)
        Journal (recent issue)
        Journal (older or discontinued title)
        Newspaper
        U.S. Document
        Pamphlet
        Non-book materials
        Microform
        Other, as appropriate to the institution

This list will include items which require the student to demonstrate his knowledge of selected filing rules such as: initial articles are ignored in filing, abbreviations are filed as if spelled out, Mc is filed as if spelled Mac, numerals are filed as if spelled out.

b.   The student knows how to use reference tools basic to all subject areas.

E1.   In a specified time period, the student can identify major reference tools (encyclopedia, dictionary, index) in a specified field using a guide to the literature such as Sheehy's *Guide to Reference Books.*

E2.   In a specified time period, the student can list five periodical titles (and the indexes which cover them) in a specified subject field using a directory such as *Ulrich's International Periodical Directory.*

E3.   In a specified time period, the student will list five titles available on a specified topic using a bibliography such as *Subject Guide to Books in Print*, Library of Congress, *Books: Subjects.*

E4.   Given a topic with which the student is unfamiliar, in a specified time period, he will locate a general introduction to that topic and at least two references to further information using an encyclopedia. The topic as stated should require the use of the encyclopedia's index to locate relevant materials.

E5.   Given a list of topics and a list of indexes (such as *Readers' Guide, Social Science Index, Humanities Index, Applied Science and*

---

*An asterisk beside an item indicates that the exact value indicated is not recommended; it is only suggested.

Technology Index, Public Affairs Information Service) which best covers each topic. At least 85%* of the students' selections should be correct.

E6. Given a sample entry, the student will correctly identify selected elements of a typical periodical index entry in a specified period of time. These elements will include: title of article, title of journal, volume, date, author, pages.

E7. Given the author and title of a book, the student will locate a review of that book in a specified time period using a book review index such as *Book Review Digest*, and *Book Review Index.*

E8. Given a specific topic of current interest, in a specified time period, the student will locate two newspaper articles on that topic using a newspaper index such as the *New York Times Index.*

E9. Given a topic of recent concern to the federal government, the student can locate citations to information issued by both the Executive and Congressional branches using the *CIS Index* and/or the *Monthly Catalog* in a specified time period.

E10. Given a specific need for statistical information on the US, the student can locate the needed statistics and identify the agency publication from which the statistic was taken using *Statistical Abstract of the United States* in a specified period of time.

c. The student knows how information is organized in his own field of interest and how to use its basic reference tools.

E1. The student will identify the major channels of scholarly communication within his/her own field of interest and formats in which this communication appears in the literature.

E2. The student will list the type of reference tool which best controls each format of the literature in his/her field of interest.

E3. Given a list of types of reference tools, the student will list at least one title of each type within his own field of interest; or where a specific type of tool is lacking, will so indicate.

E4. Given a list of ten key reference tools in his own field of interest, the student will specify the type of information each contains and/or the type of question each will answer.

E5. Given a sample entry from each of ten key reference tools in his own field of interest, the student will correctly identify collected elements of the entry.

E6. Given a list of prominent current authors and/or topics in his own field of interest, the student will be able to identify at least one journal article by/on each within the past year, using appropriate indexes to the field.

d. The student can plan and implement an efficient search strategy using:

E1. Given a complex topic in his/her own field of interest, in a specified time period the student will indicate, orally or in writing:
  (1) The major subtopics involved;
  (2) Whether primary and/or secondary sources are required by each subtopic, and their general nature;
  (3) The most probable type of reference tool to identify the relevant sources for each subtopic;

(4) The most relevant library and/or nonlibrary collections and resources for the study of the topic, whether on or off campus;

(5) An efficient order of consulting the suggested types of tools, moving from general to specific, and including, as appropriate, both informational and bibliographic tools, retrospective and current, which results in relevant literature;

(6) An alternative order of procedure and/or alternative type of tools to derive the needed information.

e. The student is able to evaluate materials and select those appropriate to his needs.

E1. Given a topic within his major field of interest, in a specified time period, the student will compile a quality bibliography using an efficient search strategy and keep a diary of his search. A librarian and/or classroom faculty member will judge the quality of the bibliography on the following factors:

(1) 80%* of the entries shall meet one or more of the following criteria: (a) be written by recognized authorities in the field. (b) be represented in standard bibliographies on the topic. (c) appear in a recognized journal in the field.

(2) bibliographic format will conform to accepted standards in that subject field.

A librarian will judge the efficiency of the search strategy as evidenced in the diary. The diary should evidence:

(1) The student clearly defined his topic before or during the initial stages of the search.

(2) The student considered and effectively used alternative search terms throughout his search.

(3) The student consulted an encyclopedia or handbook or other general source to obtain standard data or information on his topic early in his search.

(4) The student searched for and used available bibliographies on his topic.

(5) The student searched relevant indexes, or abstracts to update his information.

(6) The student used the subject card catalog.

(7) The student used bibliographies and/or footnotes in relevant materials found during his search.

(8) The student, where appropriate, used book reviews, biographical aids or other sources to help him evaluate materials.

(9) The student made accurate complete bibliographic notes and avoided repeated searches to locate or check citations.

(10) The student located materials of interest to him outside the library.

(11) The student consulted librarians and faculty members for aid and suggestions whenever appropriate.

Notes

1. Bibliographic instruction is defined here to mean instruction in the bibliographic apparatus available in the library and their effective and

efficient use. While an orientation program which covers a particular physical facility is necessary at each academic institution, the ACRL Bibliographic Instruction Section is concerned primarily with the use of the bibliographic structure housed in the library.

2. General objective is the overall goal of the program; terminal objectives break the general objectives down into specific meaningful units; and enabling objectives define the specific knowledge or skills which are necessary to achieve the terminal objectives. The terminology comes from the Commission on Instruction Technology's report in *To Improve Learning* v. 2 (Bowker, 1970), p. 944.

3. *Improve Learning* v. 2 (Bowker, 1970), p. 944. Julie S. Vargas, *Writing Worthwhile Behavioral Objectives* (New York: Harper, 1972), p. 175.

APPENDIX D
THINK TANK RECOMMENDATIONS
FOR BIBLIOGRAPHIC INSTRUCTION

Almost five years ago the Bibliographic Instruction Section (BIS) was formed. Immediately it became one of ACRL's largest and most active sections, a reflection of the growth and development experienced within bibliographic instruction itself. At its preconference in July 1981, a Think Tank of "first generation" bibliographic instruction librarians* was organized to discuss the present state and future direction of what now may be considered the bibliographic instruction movement.

The result of the Think Tank's deliberations is a series of recommendations for the "second generation" of bibliographic instruction librarians, which is here presented. It is not intended to be a definitive statement of all issues facing instruction theorists and librarians; rather it focuses on what the Think Tank members agreed are the most pressing issues facing bibliographic instruction as it moves into what is expected to be a period of maturation.

There are two recurring themes in the documents: 1) "building bridges" – to the rest of the profession, to the larger academic community, and the library schools – and 2) consolidating the discipline by fostering research, publication, critical analysis, and development of an underlying pedagogy of bibliographic instruction. It is the hope of the Think Tank members that by sharing their deliberations and conclusions, their work will stimulate widespread discussion and contribute to the growth of bibliographic instruction and to the increase in the quality of library service to the academic community.

*Paula Walker, University of Washington; Carla Stoffle, University of Wisconsin-Parkside; Anne Roberts, State University of New York at Albany; Brian Nielsen, Northwestern University; Donald Kenney, Virginia Polytechnic Institute and State University; Frances Hopkins, Temple University; and Joanne Euster, San Francisco State University, facilitator.

Reprinted by permission of the American Library Association from *College & Research Libraries News* 42 (11): 169-71 (Dec. 1981); copyright © 1981 by the American Library Association.

I.   Integration of Bibliographic Instruction
into the Library Profession

The Think Tank members viewed bibliographic instruction as a client-centered approach to library service which has implications for the redesign of all library activities. They rejected the traditional notion of the academic library as a mere adjunct to the education program, which led to the establishment of a type of reference service borrowed almost unconsciously from the public library model. They rejected as well the notion of the library-college, in which the academic library loses its special identity within the institution. The Think Tank further rejected the notion of bibliographic instruction as a secondary activity of library reference departments, and instead viewed it as the very heart of the reference process. Bibliographic instruction advocates are concerned with much more than how reference departments conduct their work. Because they believe that academic libraries should have a "central" role in the general education of all undergraduates and should "actively" support education within the academic disciplines, bibliographic instruction librarians are coming to define themselves as a political movement within academic librarianship. Recommendations:

A.   Sharing the values which underlie the bibliographic instruction movement should become the means for continuing development of that movement. This can be done by creating support groups for those both "in the trenches" now and those in the "first generation" who have moved into other jobs not identified with bibliographic instruction.

B.   As bibliographic instruction concerns arise in other areas of librarianship, the responsibility should be taken to communicate those concerns openly and loudly. Specifically:

   1.   Leaders in BIS should turn greater attention to ongoing developments *outside* BIS in order to identify decision points that could affect the future of the movement.

   2.   Instruction librarians should strive to influence the future directions of ACRL and ALA by becoming involved in sections and committees other than BIS, by seeking office in the associations, and by openly questioning and reviewing candidates for ACRL and ALA offices.

   3.   Attention should be paid to the areas of technological change, management of academic libraries, and the economic conditions of academic libraries and the processes of information transfer.

II.   Integration of Bibliographic Instruction
and the Whole of Academic Librarianship
into Higher Education

The library is an integral component of an academic institution. It affects and is affected by external factors which impinge on higher education as a whole, such as the economy, the birth pool, and public attitudes toward education; and by internal factors as well, including the organization of the individual institution's teaching methods and emphasis, curriculum, and quality of faculty expertise. Recommendations:

In order to develop successful library service programs and integrate such programs into the curriculum of the institution, especially programs of bibliographic instruction, it is necessary to do the following:

A. Define the purpose of the academic library, communicate this purpose to the higher education community, and investigate useful programmatic structures and activities for fulfilling that purpose.

B. Develop mechanisms to ensure that academic librarians understand the complex power structure of colleges and universities, learn how to analyze the governance and power structures of their own institutions, and learn ways to achieve desired objectives using those structures.

C. Develop a better understanding of the history and nature of higher education in general.

D. Develop means to help academic librarians become aware of and take advantage of changes taking place in higher education. Areas for concern include the renaissance of the general education movement, the concerns for the maintenance of quality teaching, educational standards and basic skills, changes in the nature of the student body, and financial retrenchment.

E. Become aware of and understand the socialization and priorities of faculty. Use this information to improve the library's involvement in the teaching/learning process.

F. Develop means to capture the attention of college and university administrators and make them aware of the potential of academic libraries and librarians. Demonstrate an understanding of their problems, and show how librarians, particularly bibliographic instruction librarians, can help. Possibilities include publishing articles in higher education publications, attendance at programs of higher education associations, and conducting workshops.

G. Encourage academic librarians to join and participate in discipline associations. Provide a list of discipline association meetings (time, location) yearly and especially encourage librarians in that geographic area to attend and/or prepare papers.

H. Review the basic textbooks of all disciplines. Evaluate what they say and do not say about libraries. Become vocal with publishers about changes needed.

III. Integrating Library Use Skills,
Bibliographic Concepts,
and Available Technology

Bibliographic instruction is intended to teach students to make intelligent, independent decisions about library use. To be able to use the card catalog, reference sources, or computer terminals to retrieve information on very specialized topics, or to recognize that libraries are classification systems to organize the materials, are fundamental skills that each student should possess. Reduced funding means fewer materials and professional staff are available to library users. It is through effective bibliographic instructional programs that users can be taught to make the most of the available research materials and to exploit all resources at hand.

The ability to retrieve information online needs to be fully incorporated into the instructional program both in terms of the capabilities and the limitations of various information systems. However, in order to teach users to make maximum use of the collection and to develop interpretive and evaluative skills concerning information, it is necessary that instructional programs go beyond the typical "bag of tricks" so prevalent in many instructional programs. Studying and observing the methodologies of other disciplines could enrich bibliographic instruction programs. Adapting and adopting various teaching approaches and methods from these disciplines would enable instructional programs to maintain their vitality and appeal. Recommendations:

It is necessary for all bibliographic instruction programs to integrate skills, concepts, and technology. This can best be achieved if the following goals become guiding principles:

A. All sound instruction is based on the imparting of the basic tenets of a body of knowledge; all instruction should be conceptually based.

B. Technological changes should be adopted to enhance the methods utilized with library instruction. Developing technology, however, should not be viewed as reducing the need for instruction programs.

C. Teaching methodologies of other disciplines should be studied and observed to adapt to bibliographic instruction.

IV. Relationships with the Schools
of Library Science

There is a general agreement among bibliographic instruction librarians that we need to build bridges with the library schools and their faculties, and encourage them to offer courses in bibliographic instruction so that their graduates possess the skills and specialties that are needed for library programs. Library schools should be encouraged to restructure and refocus their programs to be more responsive to the library market. The leadership in the library profession comes from the practitioners as well as from library school faculty, and instruction librarians, as practitioners, need to exert this leadership on the curriculum, content, and direction of library schools. Recommendations:

A. Propose a model program for the library school curriculum for bibliographic instruction. The model program should include a statement of rationale, course content, and materials for the teaching of bibliographic instruction.

B. Maintain a roster of librarians prepared to teach and act as speakers and resource people for courses, workshops, and conferences in bibliographic instruction. Develop a list of library school faculty who are willing to team teach or work with instruction librarians in the area of bibliographic instruction.

C. Identify library school courses and other graduate school courses which relate to library instruction in method and/or content. Identify library science and other faculty who may have an interest in bibliographic instruction and act as a resource to them for bibliographic instruction information.

D. Promote and publicize bibliographic instruction in library schools by recognizing those which offer courses. Reward those schools by hiring their students and honoring their faculty.

E. Seek collaboration with library school faculty on research projects. Work with them in other professional activities such as conferences and symposia. Provide them with an environment for internship and laboratories in academic libraries.

F. Encourage library school faculty to be active in ALA and ACRL, as opposed to focusing their energies solely on the library educators' group.

G. Stop sending surveys to library schools asking about their bibliographic instruction curricula. Instead, spend the time and effort on identifying bibliographic instruction related courses by working with students and faculty in the above recommended manner.

V. Importance of Research

A. Bibliographic instruction should be based on knowledge of the social and intellectual characteristics of the academic disciplines which give rise to their different patterns of scholarly, bibliographic, and encyclopedic literature. Recommendations:

1. Preparation of studies by bibliographic instruction practitioners which review, synthesize, and apply to bibliographic instruction (a) analyses by scholars of the goals and methodologies of their own disciplines, and (b)

analyses by external researchers of the intellectual history, emergent sub-fields, and publication and citation patterns of the academic disciplines.

2. Disseminate such studies to the authors cited and invite those authors to participate in BIS conferences, in order to promote their awareness and criticism of applications of their work to bibliographic instruction.

B. Library research competence has traditionally depended largely on tacit knowledge acquired through the process of socialization to a discipline. While library use has been studied mainly through surveys of user groups and compilation of statistics on services rendered, the behavior of individual users is still largely a mystery. Instruction librarians should make explicit (and thus teachable) the tacit knowledge of experienced researchers and determine the concepts and techniques which should be taught. Recommendations:

1. Record and analyze the library research behavior of scientists and scholars in different disciplines as they move from initial formulation of a research problem through various uses of the literature to the final production of new knowledge.

2. Study the research efforts of students to identify and analyze prevalent patterns of ignorance and misunderstanding.

C. Competency in library research should be a fundamental goal of education. Effective bibliographic instruction contributes to students' understanding of the nature of learning and scholarship, directly supports their coursework, and helps prepare them for self-directed life-long learning.
   Recommendations:

1. Bibliographic instruction needs no more justification than instruction in composition or any of the liberal arts, and evaluation studies aimed at justifying its existence are unnecessary.

2. Evaluation studies should be used primarily to improve the effectiveness of existing bibliographic instruction programs and should rarely require dissemination beyond the institution where the data was gathered.

D. Few bibliographic instruction practitioners work in circumstances conducive to ongoing research, and every effort should, therefore, be made to expand the number of researchers in the field. Recommendations:

1. Library and information science faculty in the field of scholarly communication should be made aware of the applications of their work to bibliographic instruction, and their collaboration should be sought in defining research problems suitable for their doctoral students.

VI.   Importance of Publication

Literature should serve as a common base for communication among all librarians involved in bibliographic instruction, including academic, school, public, and special libraries. Recommendations:

A.   The bibliographic instruction movement should publish a journal of its own which:

1.   Maintains an editorial policy directed toward the concerns of bibliographic instruction;

2.   Contains substantive articles of high quality;

3.   Includes review articles of the bibliographic instruction literature and evaluative reviews of teaching materials and methods from other literature;

4.   Is graphically well designed and professional in appearance.

B.   Librarians involved in the bibliographic instruction movement should publish articles in a wide variety of journals in order to disseminate the latest information on bibliographic instruction, to share current research, and to generate scholarly discussion.

1.   Journals concentrating on teaching methods are published in many academic subject fields. A list of these journals should be prepared and made available to bibliographic instruction librarians.

2.   Journals, such as *Change* and the *Chronicle of Higher Education*, are read by administrators. Articles on bibliographic instruction are needed in these publications to reach key people who may not read journals concerning librarianship or teaching methods.

C.   Resource materials for teaching library skills and for learning bibliographic instruction methods should be collected, critically evaluated, and made available on a selective basis.

1.   Materials for use in teaching librarians how to do bibliographic instruction (such as textbooks, course outlines, etc.) should be published.

2.   A collection of model exercises and other teaching materials should be maintained.

3.   A means should be devised by which materials collected and/or published are evaluated and those evaluations shared with librarians utilizing the materials.

D. An ongoing review should be conducted of the research literature within library/information science and in other academic disciplines having implications for bibliographic instruction (e.g., in scholarly communication, economics of publishing, learning theory). This information should be disseminated to instruction practitioners.

APPENDIX E
ORGANIZING AND MANAGING A
LIBRARY INSTRUCTION PROGRAM:
CHECKLISTS*

BIBLIOGRAPHIC INSTRUCTION CHECKLIST
ELEMENTS OF A MODEL
LIBRARY INSTRUCTION PROGRAM

I.   Preliminary planning

    _____A. Studentbody enrollment in college
- _____1. 0-3,000
- _____2. 3,001-6,000
- _____3. 6,001-10,000
- _____4. 10,001-20,000
- _____5. 20,001 and over

    _____B. Level of students in college
- _____1. First two years only
- _____2. Four-year undergraduate
- _____3. Graduate only
- _____4. Undergraduate and graduate

    _____C. Area of study of student who will participate in library instruction program
- _____1. Liberal arts or "generalists"
- _____2. Vocational and/or technical
- _____3. Professional, e.g. law, medical, dental
- _____4. Graduate research major

    _____D. What portion of studentbody will participate
- _____1. All those enrolled in a given course
- _____2. All those enrolled in a given program
- _____3. Potentially everyone, i.e. whomever is enrolled in a course with a faculty member who participates
- _____4. Everyone

---

*Reprint, ED# IR 176731.

_____E. Has planning time been given to
      _____1. Quiet thinking
      _____2. Discussions with
            _____a) Faculty
            _____b) Librarians
            _____c) Students

_____F. Has faculty input been actively solicited

_____G. Has there been consultation with education specialist for discussion of
      _____1. Teaching techniques
      _____2. Methodology
      _____3. Curriculum planning

_____H. What form(s) will library instruction take
      _____1. Point-of-use instruction with librarian explaining tool to student
      _____2. Point-of-use instruction using an audiovisual aid
      _____3. Voluntary course-related sessions at request of faculty
      _____4. Required course-related sessions
      _____5. Credit course
      _____6. Self-paced course(s) on volunteer basis
      _____7. Required self-paced course(s)

II. Objectives
_____A. Formulated after consultation with
      _____1. Librarians only
      _____2. Faculty only
      _____3. Students only
      _____4. Librarians and faculty
      _____5. Faculty and students
      _____6. Librarians, faculty and students

_____B. Related to library's service goals

_____C. Related to college or program curriculum

_____D. Related to college or program requirements

_____E. Related to course curriculum

_____F. Clearly delineated

III.   Administration and staffing
_____A.   Who will administer the library instruction program
         _____1.   a coordinator of instruction hired for that purpose
         _____2.   a designated member of public service
         _____3.   rotating responsibility
         _____4.   other

_____B.   Who will teach in library instruction program
         _____1.   All librarians on staff
         _____2.   Librarians who volunteer
         _____3.   One or more librarians whose assignment is library
                      instruction

_____C.   Are there enough library instructors participating
         _____1.   To meet the "start-up" demand
         _____2.   To meet the potential demand

_____D.   Are participating librarians being given released time
         _____1.   to plan curriculum
         _____2.   to develop materials
         _____3.   to teach

IV.   Syllabus/Curriculum
_____A.   Have discussions taken place among the library staff and
              particularly reference librarians regarding the precise
              subject matter that should be covered

_____B.   Has faculty input been sought regarding subject matter

_____C.   Will the curriculum of the program help to meet the stated
              objectives

_____D.   Is the curriculum relevant to the information needs of the
              students

_____E.   Is the curriculum realistic in length and depth for the
              potential student participants

V.   Publicity
_____A.   To library staff
         _____1.   Through announcements and discussions in meeting
         _____2.   Through newsletters, brochures, flyers, posters, etc.
         _____3.   Through one-to-one discussion

     _____B.   To faculty
           _____1.   To those who teach courses involved with library instruction
           _____2.   To those who teach any subject
           _____3.   In faculty meetings; all-college or departmental
           _____4.   By sending person letters
           _____5.   By telephone contact
           _____6.   By one-to-one when faculty member is in library
           _____7.   By one-to-one through faculty office visits by librarians

     _____C.   To students
           _____1.   By signs/posters in library
           _____2.   By hand-outs
           _____3.   Through student newspaper
           _____4.   Through one-to-one discussion in or outside the library

VI.   Materials
     _____A.   Have teaching aids been considered

     _____B.   Have teaching aids been developed
           _____1.   Print
           _____2.   Non-print

     _____C.   Have student hand-outs been duplicated in sufficient number

     _____D.   Have student work sheets or exercises been duplicated in sufficient number

VII.   Budget
     _____A.   Staff: full time, part time, released time
           _____1.   Coordinator _____
           _____2.   Library instructors _____
           _____3.   Developing materials _____

     _____B.   Materials
           _____1.   Supplies; e.g. paper, paints, lettering sets, etc.
           _____2.   Audiovisual supplies
           _____3.   Audiovisual equipment
           _____4.   Reproduction costs

VIII. Space

_____A. Classroom

_____B. Classroom within library

_____C. Group gathering space within library

_____D. Consulting space within library

IX. Evaluation techniques

_____A. Of what students who have participated have learned
     _____1. pre-testing
     _____2. post-testing
     _____3. quizzes
     _____4. discussion

_____B. By students of the course or session

_____C. By faculty of the course or session

_____D. By librarians, teaching and non-teaching, of the program as they see it through students who have participated

Patricia W. Silvernail

BIBLIOGRAPHIC INSTRUCTION CHECKLIST ASSESSING STUDENT NEEDS

I. Type of institution
_____A. Two-year college

_____B. Four-year college

_____C. University

_____D. Specialized: technical, professional, etc.

_____E. Other _____

II. Student profile
    A. Age group
     _____1. Under 18
     _____2. 18-22
     _____3. 22-29
     _____4. 30 or over

B. Type of courses
_____1. Undergraduate; major _____
           _____a) Freshman
           _____b) Sophomore
           _____c) Junior
           _____d) Senior
_____2. Graduate, subject _____
           _____a) Masters
           _____b) Doctorate
           _____c) Other _____
_____3. Continuing education: interests _____
_____4. Other _____

C. Residence
_____1. Lives on campus
_____2. Lives near campus (within 20 minutes)
_____3. Commutes over 20 minutes

D. Registered for courses
_____1. Daytime during week
_____2. Evening
_____3. Weekends
_____4. Any combination of above _____

III. Student attitude toward library
_____A. Enthusiastic

_____B. Positive

_____C. Comfortable in library setting

_____D. Indifferent

_____E. Intimidated or embarrassed

_____F. Negative

IV. Past experience with library instruction
_____A. Elementary school library

_____B. Public library

_____C. High School Library

_____D. College or university library

_____E. Other _____

_____F. No previous library instruction

V.   Types of library instruction student has had within the present institution
_____A.   Library tour

_____B.   Orientation: brief introduction to the concept of library and its facilities

_____C.   Handouts: Floor plans, bibliographies, library handbook, research strategies, etc.

_____D.   Point-of-use instruction in library

_____E.   Audiovisual programs

_____F.   Classroom instruction

_____G.   Other _____

_____H.   None

VI.   Student expectations of library
_____A.   Leisure reading

_____B.   Research use of books

_____C.   Research use of periodicals

_____D.   Reserve readings

_____E.   Study hall use

_____F.   Assistance in locating information
_____1.   Short term
_____2.   Long term

_____G.   Reward of better grades when research becomes easier

_____H.   Reward of gratification when able to pursue research on his/her own

VII.   Type of assignment student may have to complete
_____A.   Short research paper

_____B.   Term paper

_____C.   Use of research material on a particular topic

_____D.   Reserve readings already assigned

_____E.   Other _____

VIII.   Student rationale or motivation for attending voluntary library instruction program

    _____A.   To get general background of library resources

    _____B.   To become familiar with new subject areas

    _____C.   To get help on a specific information need

    _____D.   To follow suggestion of faculty

IX.   Ways in which library instruction may be carried out for this student

    _____A.   Library tour

    _____B.   Group instruction in classroom by librarian

    _____C.   Group instruction in library by librarian

    _____D.   One-to-one instruction by librarian

    _____E.   Slide/tape presentation

    _____F.   Handouts

    _____G.   Other _____

X.   Means of assessing student progress in bibliographic instruction

    _____A.   Oral
        _____1.   Conversation between librarian and student
        _____2.   Conversation between librarian and classroom instructor

    _____B.   Review of final papers by librarian

    _____C.   Written questionnaire or survey

    _____D.   Other._____

Timothea McDonald

BIBLIOGRAPHIC INSTRUCTION CHECKLIST
ASSESSING CLASSROOM INSTRUCTOR INTEREST
IN BIBLIOGRAPHIC INSTRUCTION
THROUGH AN INTERVIEW

I.   How would you evaluate the students' use of the library?
        _____A.   Heavy

        _____B.   Moderate

        _____C.   Light

II.   Do you make assignments that require students to use the library?
        _____A.   If so, what kind of assignments are they?

        _____B.   If not, what are the reasons for not making such
                 assignments?

III.   What skills do you see as most important for students to have in order to
        use the library?

IV.   How do you think library skills are best developed?
        _____A.   Do students pick them up naturally and on their own, as
                 they need the library for various courses?

        _____B.   Is library orientation (brief tour and introduction)
                 helpful?

        _____C.   Should library resources and research skills be taught as
                 needed within given courses?
                 _____1.   By faculty? If so, how? Do you teach these now?
                          How?
                 _____2.   By librarians? If so, how would you like to see this
                          carried out? Bring to faculty's attention several
                          possible alternatives, such as workbooks, one-hour
                          class presentations, etc.

        _____D.   Should library-use instruction be completely independent
                 of regular course work? For example, a separate, one-to-
                 three hour course in bibliography and search skills or non-
                 credit mini-courses or term paper clinics could be offered
                 by library staff independent of any courses. If this is a
                 recommended approach, does the faculty member think
                 students would be sufficiently motivated to take advantage
                 of these?

                 The librarian should engage faculty in a discussion of all these
                 alternatives, and any others mentioned, and pursue the reasons
                 for any of the alternatives the faculty member recommends.

V.   How did you learn to use the library effectively as a student?

VI.   Describe your own library needs and the use you are making of our collections and services at the present time. Are there ways that the library staff could be more helpful to you in your use of the library?

Phyllis Andrews

BIBLIOGRAPHIC INSTRUCTION CHECKLIST
ASSESSING THE DEAN'S INTEREST IN BIBLIOGRAPHIC INSTRUCTION THROUGH AN INTERVIEW

I.   How would you evaluate the students' use of the library?
          _____A.   Heavy

          _____B.   Moderate

          _____C.   Light

II.   In courses you teach or have taught: have you made assignments that required students to use the library?
          _____A.   If so, what kind of assignments were they?

          _____B.   If not, what were your reasons for not making library assignments?

III.   What skills do you see as most important for students to have in order to use the library?

IV.   How do you think library skills are best developed?
          _____A.   Do students pick them up naturally and on their own, as they need the library for various courses?

          _____B.   Is library orientation (brief tour and introduction) helpful?

          _____C.   Should library resources and research skills be taught as needed within given courses?
                _____1.   By faculty? If so, how?
                _____2.   By librarians? If so, how would you like to see this carried out? Bring to Dean's attention several possible alternatives, such as workbooks, one-hour class presentations, etc.

_____D. Should library-use instruction be completely independent of regular course work? For example, a separate, one-to-three-hour course in bibliography and search skills or non-credit mini-courses or term paper clinics could be offered by library staff independent of any courses. If this is a recommended approach, does the Dean think students would be sufficiently motivated to take advantage of these?

The librarian should engage the Dean in a discussion of all these alternatives, and any others mentioned, and pursue the reasons for any of the alternatives the Dean recommends.

V.   Is the learning of library resources and search skills one of the objectives of the curriculum here?
_____A. If so, is the achievement of this objective formally articulated or informally expected to happen?

_____B. If not, would you be interested in considering the inclusion of this objective in our curriculum?

VI. In your academic life, how did you learn to use the library effectively?

VII. Describe your own library needs and the use you are making of our collections and services at the present time. Are there ways that the library staff could be more helpful to you in your use of the library?

_____

Phyllis Andrews

BIBLIOGRAPHIC INSTRUCTION CHECKLIST
ADMINISTRATION OF A PROGRAM

A bibliographic instruction component within the present library organization structure is designated:
_____A. To investigate local needs for a program

_____B. To determine feasibility of a program

_____C. To propose a program

_____D. To implement a program

_____E. To more effectively coordinate an ongoing program

II.   Program administered by

      _____A. An overall coordinator hired for that purpose

      _____B. A member of public service staff given the coordinating assignment until further notice

      _____C. Coordinator assignment is rotated among certain staff members

      _____D. Other _____

III.   The bibliographic instruction coordinator title will be _____

IV.   The bibliographic instruction program coordinator reports to

      _____A. The Head of Reference

      _____B. The Director of Public Services

      _____C. Chief Librarian or Library Director

      _____D. Other _____

V.   Librarians who will teach and/or participate

      _____A. Librarians who have been specifically designated as "instruction librarians"

      _____B. Librarians whose official designation is "reference librarian"

      _____C. Any public service librarian

      _____D. Public service librarians selected by the program coordinator for specific qualifications

      _____E. Any librarian who volunteers

      _____F. Personnel other than professional librarians

VI.   Other program responsibilities that must be assumed/assigned and carried out

      _____A. Maintaining liaison with central academic administration

      _____B. Maintaining liaison with appropriate academic departments

      _____C. Developing materials

_____D. Revising materials

_____E. Developing and maintaining a resource center

_____F. Other _____

_____

Kay Rottsolk

BIBLIOGRAPHIC INSTRUCTION CHECKLIST
DEVELOPING OBJECTIVES

I. Educational objectives will be used
    _____A. To improve curriculum

    _____B. To increase student achievement

    _____C. To facilitate program evaluation

II. Kinds of objectives:
    _____A. General objectives for
        _____1. Studentbody of college
        _____2. All students in a course
        _____3. Individual students in any course

    _____B. Terminal objectives representing units of behavior included under general objectives

    _____C. Enabling objectives representing knowledge or skills to be mastered if student is to attain terminal objectives

III. Characteristics of well-constructed enabling objectives
    _____A. Outcome (behavior) can be evaluated because it is observable and measureable
        _____1. Such vague terms as these are avoided:
            a) To know ...
            b) To understand ...
            c) To appreciate ...
            d) To grasp the significance ...
            e) To enjoy ...
            f) To believe ...

_____2. Descriptive terms referring to specific outcomes are used:
- a) To write ...
- b) To recite ...
- c) To identify ...
- d) To differentiate ...
- e) To solve ...
- f) To construct ...
- g) To list ...
- h) To compare ...

_____B. Conditions under which the behavior is to occur are specified, using such specifications as are listed below:
- _____1. Given a list of ...
- _____2. Given any reference of the learner's choice ...
- _____3. Given a standard set of tools ...
- _____4. Without the aid of references ...
- _____5. Without the aid of a slide rule ...
- _____6. Without the aid of tools ...

_____C. A criterion statement, or standard of performance, indicating a minimum acceptable performance is included for each enabling objective, i.e.:
- _____1. A time limit,
- _____2. Minimum number of current responses, or
- _____3. Minimum percentage of current responses, or
- _____4. Minimum proportion of current responses

Murray Wortzel

BIBLIOGRAPHIC INSTRUCTION CHECKLIST
INSTRUCTIONAL MODES

I. Factors to consider in selecting a mode
- _____A. Student need in terms of immediate/delayed response
- _____B. Depth of instruction required by student to meet information need
- _____C. Amount of time student has for participation
- _____D. Effectiveness of mode in terms of retention
- _____E. Preparation time required of instructor
- _____F. Allowable student/instructor ratio
- _____G. Extent to which instruction must relate to classroom coursework
- _____H. Ease of revision/update of materials
- _____I. Adaptability to evaluation techniques

II.　Modes of instruction
　　　_____A.　Reference instruction: one-to-one instruction initiated by an inquiry at the reference desk
　　　　　_____1.　Purpose
　　　　　　　_____a)　To enable student to use tools to answer immediate information needs
　　　　　　　_____b)　To enable student to learn search techniques for the future
　　　　　_____2.　Teaching method: Explanation and demonstration
　　　　　_____3.　Instructional materials
　　　　　　　_____a)　Reference tools
　　　　　　　_____b)　Search strategy guides
　　　　　　　_____c)　Bibliographies
　　　　　　　_____d)　Other _____
　　　　　_____4.　Sessions
　　　　　　　_____a)　One session, less than one hour
　　　　　　　_____b)　One session, an hour or longer
　　　　　　　_____c)　Several sessions
　　　　　_____5.　Size of group: One student
　　　　　_____6.　Non-credit

　　　_____B.　Tutorial: In-depth instruction in the use of bibliographic materials relevant to student's particular interest
　　　　　_____1.　Purpose: To enable student
　　　　　　　_____a)　To acquire expertise in search techniques
　　　　　　　_____b)　To use major bibliographic tools in his/her area of major interest
　　　　　_____2.　Teaching method
　　　　　　　_____a)　One library instructor to one student working on an on-going basis
　　　　　　　_____b)　Guided or programmed self-paced study
　　　　　_____3.　Instructional materials
　　　　　　　_____a)　Course syllabus
　　　　　　　_____b)　Textbook
　　　　　　　_____c)　Library guides
　　　　　　　_____d)　Workbook or programmed instruction
　　　　　　　_____e)　Search problems
　　　　　　　_____f)　Bibliographies
　　　　　　　_____g)　Pre-test/post-test
　　　　　　　_____h)　Other _____
　　　　　_____4.　Extended sessions over 4-16 weeks
　　　　　_____5.　Size of group: One student
　　　　　_____6.　Credit
　　　　　　　_____a)　non-credit
　　　　　　　_____b)　credit: Number of hours: _____

　　　_____C.　Course: In-depth instruction in the use of bibliographic materials relevant to either a general interdisciplinary survey or a particular subject area

_____1. Purpose: To enable student
        _____a) To acquire expertise in search techniques
        _____b) To use major interdisciplinary bibliographic tools
        _____c) To use major bibliographic tools in his/her own subject area
_____2. Teaching method
        _____a) Lecture: Explanations and demonstrations
        _____b) Search problems or exercises necessitating student use of library
        _____c) Audiovisual programs
        _____d) Other _____
_____3. Instructional materials
        _____a) Course syllabus
        _____b) Textbook
        _____c) Library guides
        _____d) Workbook or programmed instruction
        _____e) Search problems
        _____f) Bibliographies
        _____g) Pre-test/post-test
        _____h) Other _____
_____4. Sessions: Regular, 8 to 16 weeks
_____5. Size of group: 5-15 students
_____6. Two to 4 hours

_____D. Workshops: Introduction to basic sources of information in a given subject area or format, e.g. documents, software, microforms
_____1. Purpose
        _____a) To acquaint student with major bibliographic tools
        _____b) To acquaint student with basic search techniques
        _____c) To meet needs of a course
_____2. Teaching methods
        _____a) Lecture: Explanation and demonstration
        _____b) Hands-on experience in library
_____3. Instructional materials
        _____a) Library guides to sources
        _____b) Search problems
        _____c) Bibliographies
        _____d) Other _____
_____4. One session, one to two hours long
_____5. Size of group: Five to fifteen students
_____6. Non-credit

_____E. Point-of-use: Instructions on how to use a particular bibliographic tool. The instruction is located at the tool

    _____1. Purpose: To enable a student to learn to use a particular tool without the aid of a librarian

    _____2. Teaching method: Prepared passive instrument in

       _____a) written format

       _____b) audiovisual format

       _____c) kit form

    _____3. Single or repeated sessions as needed

    _____4. Size of group: One student

    _____5. Non-credit

_____F. Tour: General introduction to building, library, personnel, services

    _____1. Purpose

       _____a) To expose student to the library

       _____b) To evoke a positive impression of the library

    _____2. Teaching method: Lecture

    _____3. Instructional materials

       _____a) Handbook

       _____b) Floor plan

       _____c) Guide to services

       _____d) Other _____

    _____4. One session

    _____5. Size of group: One to twenty students

    _____6. Non-credit

John Tongate

BIBLIOGRAPHIC INSTRUCTION CHECKLIST
DEVELOPING INSTRUCTIONAL MATERIALS

I. Rationale: Instructional materials are being considered for use

_____A. to reach a larger number of students

_____B. to provide alternatives to present forms of instruction

_____C. to supplement the instruction already being given

_____D. to provide students with an end product from a library instruction session (i.e. bibliographies)

_____E. to provide instruction to those who cannot be reached in traditional manner

_____F. to ease the problem of a limited instructional staff

_____G. to save on total preparation time

II.   Types of material being considered for the instructional program
_____1.   handbook
_____2.   self-guided tour
_____3.   workbook
_____4.   bibliography
_____5.   topical guides
_____6.   slide/tape program
_____7.   slide set
_____8.   video tape
_____9.   filmstrip
_____10.   film

III.   Costs

A.   How much professional and/or staff time is needed to develop
_____1.   guides
_____2.   handbooks
_____3.   self-guided tours
_____4.   workbook
_____5.   bibliographies
_____6.   slide/tape program
_____7.   video tape

B.   Can the library obtain the hardware (projectors, screens, tape recorders, etc.) for use with
_____1.   slide programs
_____2.   audio programs
_____3.   slide/tape programs
_____4.   films
_____5.   video tape
_____6.   transparencies

C.   Cost to library for instructional material (including time, materials and reproduction costs):
_____1.   Total cost for production or purchase:
_____a)   guides _____
_____b)   handbook _____
_____c)   self-guided tour _____
_____d)   workbook _____
_____e)   bibliography _____
_____f)   slide/tape program _____
_____g)   video tape _____

    _____2. Cost per student (divide total cost by projected number of students):

       _____a) guides _____

       _____b) handbook _____

       _____c) self-guided tour _____

       _____d) workbook _____

       _____e) bibliography _____

       _____f) slide/tape program _____

       _____g) video tape _____

    _____3. Cost per year to update materials

       _____a) guides _____

       _____b) handbook _____

       _____c) self-guided tour _____

       _____d) workbook _____

       _____e) bibliography _____

       _____f) slide/tape program _____

       _____g) video tape _____

IV.   At what audience is the instructional material being aimed

    _____A. beginning college student

    _____B. visiting pre-college groups

    _____C. graduate students

    _____D. faculty

    _____E. upper-level undergraduates

    _____F. library staff

    _____G. combination of groups

V.   Evaluation

    A. Does the instructional material

    _____1. fit in with the perceived needs of the present or anticipated instructional program

    _____2. fit within the library budget

    _____3. require an inordinate amount of time to develop

    _____4. require special equipment not presently available

    _____5. pay for itself

    _____6. make library instruction more effective

    B. Are the instructional materials

    _____1. accurate

    _____2. of good technical quality (color, sound, etc.)

    _____3. attractive

_____4.　easy to use
　　　　　_____a)　are directions clear
　　　　　_____b)　does it involve the use of equipment
_____5.　durable

_____

Beverly L. Renford

BIBLIOGRAPHIC INSTRUCTION CHECKLIST
PROGRAM TO TEACH LIBRARIANS TO TEACH

I.　Purposes and goals
　　_____A.　To encourage librarians to increase their knowledge about teaching methods and innovations in education

　　_____B.　To establish standards for teaching among the various participants in the program

　　_____C.　To develop within librarians the ability to calculate the parameters and complexity of the material to be covered with a group of students

　　_____D.　To enable librarians to feel comfortable and secure in their dealings with faculty

　　_____E.　To give librarians an opportunity to share their knowledge and enthusiasm with students and staff

　　_____F.　To develop a core of librarians who cannot only teach bibliographic classes, but who can teach other librarians to teach as well

II.　Prerequisites for the program
　　_____A.　A group of librarians interested and willing to take part

　　_____B.　At least one person on the staff to coordinate the program, and possibly do the training

　　_____C.　An administration willing to support the program with:
　　　　_____1.　At least minimal funding
　　　　　　_____a)　Hire additional staff for instruction
　　　　　　_____b)　Commit released time to participating staff for preparation and teaching
　　　　_____2.　Moral support by encouraging department heads, for example, to recognize it as an important facet of the college

    _____D. Department heads throughout the system willing to:
        _____1. Release staff to enable them to take part in the program
        _____2. Allow time, once staff has completed the program, to enable them to prepare and teach classes

III.   Librarians will be trained by
    _____A. The person selected as coordinator will also be the person training the staff

    _____B. Qualified personnel from other Departments within the University or College (such as Education faculty, Communications Arts faculty, etc.) will do the training

    _____C. Someone will be hired expressly for the purpose of doing the training

    _____D. A combination of any or all of the above

IV.   Librarians who will participate in the program
    _____A. Librarians who have been specifically designated as "instruction librarians"

    _____B. Librarians whose official designation is "reference librarian"

    _____C. Any public service librarian

    _____D. Public Service librarians selected by the program coordinator for specific qualifications

    _____E. Any librarian who volunteers

    _____F. Personnel other than professional librarians

    _____G. Other _____

V.   Physical facilities that must be planned for
    _____A. Space for meeting
        _____1. Classroom
        _____2. Conference room
        _____3. Other suitable space

    _____B. Equipment
        _____1. Chalkboard, chalk and erasers
        _____2. Video camera and play back equipment
        _____3. Slide projector

_____4. Tape recorder
_____5. Overhead projector

_____C. Other teaching aids
_____1. Prepared posters
_____2. Slides
_____3. Slide tape shows
_____4. Sample materials, e.g. catalog cards, indexes

VI. Other things to consider
_____A. Approval of library supervisory personnel

_____B. Time commitment of participants

_____C. Selection of participants

_____D. Future involvement by trainees in the bibliographic instruction program

_____E. Cost of program

Joan Ormondroyd

BIBLIOGRAPHIC INSTRUCTION CHECKLIST
EVALUATION OF A PROGRAM

I. The evaluation of the bibliographic instruction program is being considered
_____A. To seek approval of the program
_____1. From outside funding agencies
_____2. From college administration
_____3. From library administration
_____4. From fellow librarians
_____5. From classroom instructors
_____6. Other _____

_____B. To provide information
_____1. Concerning effectiveness of instruction; i.e. did it teach skills desired
_____2. Concerning skills developed by students; i.e. did the students learn what was expected
_____3. Concerning attitudes of the students
_____4. Concerning application of skills taught

II. Information from the evaluation will be used
_____A. To measure attainment of objectives

_____B. To improve an existing program

_____C. To determine the need for expanding the program

_____D. Other (specify) _____

III.   The results of the evaluation will be reported to
_____A. University administration

_____B. Library administration

_____C. Librarians involved with program

_____D. Classroom instructors

_____E. Students

IV.   The evaluation tool or method will be devised by
_____A. The coordinator of the bibliographic instruction program

_____B. Bibliographic instruction librarians

_____C. Library staff

_____D. Library staff and other faculty

_____E. Other _____

V.   Input for developing the instrument will be provided by
_____A. Students

_____B. Librarians

_____C. Bibliographic instruction librarians

_____D. Classroom instructors

VI.   Evaluation format
_____A. Formal
_____1. Pre-test and post-test
_____2. Interviews with students
_____3. Interviews with classroom instructors

_____B. Informal
_____1. Comments by students
_____2. Comments by librarians

_____3. Comments by classroom instructors

_____C. Reactive
     _____1. Questionnaire to participating students
     _____2. Survey

_____D. Non-reactive
     _____1. Observation
     _____2. Statistics

VII.   Are the evaluation methods valid and reliable
     _____A. If a test
          _____1. Will students answer the question the same way consistently
          _____2. Will the answer to a question really indicate whether the student does or does not possess a particular skill or attitude

     _____B. Will the evaluation method affect the attitudes and skills of the students

     _____C. Is the evaluation device highly subject to the bias of the evaluator

Larry Hardesty

BIBLIOGRAPHIC INSTRUCTION CHECKLIST
GAINING AND MAINTAINING COLLEGIAL SUPPORT WITHIN THE LIBRARY

I.   Cooperation among library staff
    A. Commitment of non-instructional librarians to the library instructional program in terms of
      1. Sharing of goals
         _____a) commitment
         _____b) acceptance
         _____c) no commitment
         _____d) disagreement
      2. Sharing of expertise
         _____a) commitment
         _____b) acceptance
         _____c) no commitment
         _____d) disagreement
      3. Exchange of constructive criticism
         _____a) open
         _____b) restrained but happens
         _____c) no exchange

_____B. Commitment of instructional librarians to the non-instructional programs in terms of
1. Sharing of goals
_____a) commitment
_____b) acceptance
_____c) no commitment
_____d) disagreement
2. Sharing of expertise
_____a) commitment
_____b) acceptance
_____c) no commitment
_____d) disagreement
3. Exchange of constructive criticism
_____a) open
_____b) restrained but happens
_____c) no exchange

II. Participation of non-instructional librarians in the instructional program
A. Do non-instructional librarians participate in program planning
_____1. as developers of a mission and goals statement
_____2. as co-developers of a comprehensive program of instruction
_____3. as co-authors of instructional objectives

B. Do non-instructional librarians participate in program implementation
_____1. as instructional team members
_____2. as instructional developers
_____3. as subject specialists

C. Do non-instructional librarians participate in program evaluation
_____1. as members of the program review team
_____2. as monitors and critics of instructional sessions
_____3. as evaluators of data

III. Fostering communication between instructional and non-instructional librarians
A. Are views of non-instructional librarians actively sought
_____1. regularly
_____2. occasionally
_____3. never

B. Are non-instructional librarians kept informed of decisions made regarding the instructional program
_____1. regularly
_____2. occasionally
_____3. never

C. Are communication channels in the library open
_____1. open
_____2. somewhat open
_____3. closed

D. Have *formal* ways of improving the quality of communication between instructional and non-instructional staff in the library been explored
_____1. staff meetings where the instructional program and student needs are discussed
_____2. in-house staff publications
_____3. routing published articles on library instruction among all library staff members

E. Have *informal* ways of improving the quality of communication between instructional and non-instructional staff in the library been explored
_____1. one-to-one conversations with instructional librarians initiating conversations regarding library instruction with non-instructional colleagues
_____2. have non-instructional librarians been invited to help prepare publications, handouts, bibliographies, etc.

IV. Flexibility and reciprocity in staffing patterns
A. Do non-instructional staff serve in instructional service positions/roles
_____1. regularly
_____2. occasionally
_____3. never

B. Do instructional staff serve in non-instructional service positions/roles
_____1. regularly
_____2. occasionally
_____3. never

C. Are new staff hired with a view to their potential to contribute to a flexible staffing pattern
_____1. regularly
_____2. occasionally
_____3. never

Kathy Jordan

BIBLIOGRAPHIC INSTRUCTION CHECKLIST
GAINING AND MAINTAINING INSTITUTIONAL SUPPORT

I. Demonstrate the need for bibliographic instruction with
_____A. Practical examples from daily experience
_____1. with students
_____2. with faculty

_____B. Professional documentation
_____1. From the literature
_____a) of library science
_____b) of education
_____c) of other disciplines
_____2. Indicated by the proliferation of
_____a) workshops and conferences
_____b) special organizations
_____c) clearinghouses

II. Suggest a viable solution through a plan of action which includes all the
essential elements for a successful program
_____A. Statement that responsibility for education for use of
library tools rests with the professionals best trained in the
use of those tools

_____B. Utilize "Bibliographic Instruction Checklist" to facilitate
planning

_____C. Establish a tentative timetable

_____D. Develop a proposed budget

_____E. Propose progress reports on a regular basis

_____F. Include attitude questionnaire and needs assessment
surveys of
_____1. Faculty
_____2. Students

Phyllis J. Hudson

INDEX